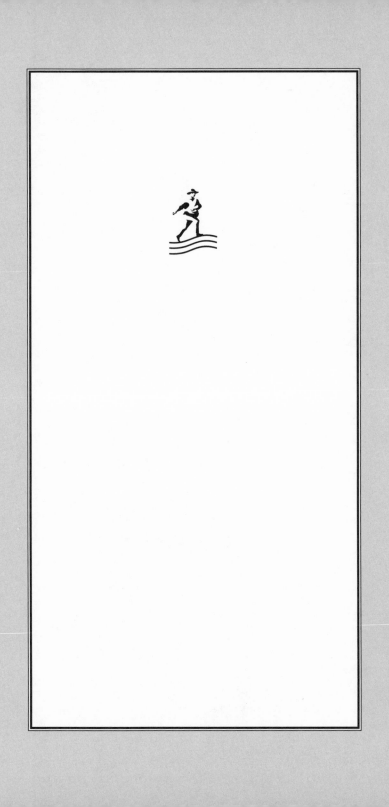

FINDING THE BOYFRIEND WITHIN

BRAD GOOCH

Simon & Schuster

SIMON & SCHUSTER
Rockefeller Center
1230 Avenue of the Americas
New York, NY 10020
Copyright © 1999 by Brad Gooch

Designed by Ruth Lee

Manufactured in the United States of America

1   3   5   7   9   10   8   6   4   2

Library of Congress Cataloging-in-Publication Data
Gooch, Brad, date.
Finding the boyfriend within / Brad Gooch.
p.   cm.
1. Gay men—Psychology. 2. Single men—Psychology.
3. Male friendship. I. Title.
HQ76.25.G66   1999
305.38'9664—dc21   98-50441   CIP

ISBN 0-684-85040-0

Special thanks to Barbara Heizer, for thoughtfully reading this book in manuscript; to Geoff Freitag, Bill Katz, Wayne Nathan, and Mary Michael Simpson for their encouragement and anecdotes; to my editor, Chuck Adams, and my agent, Joy Harris.

FINDING THE
BOYFRIEND WITHIN

INTRODUCTION

Here's the situation: I'm in my mid-forties. Everyone says I look ten years younger, more or less. I'm gay, but extremely flexible and historically not too worried, ashamed, or complicated about my predilections. (I don't remember the phrase "coming out" even going through my head when I decided to get on with my romantic life in my late teens.)

I had a lover, Howard. When I was twenty-five, and he was twenty-three, we met at an innocuous, somewhat preppy gay bar in the Village misleadingly named The Ninth Circle—there were at least a half dozen bars in Manhattan in 1978 much more deserving to be named after the final circle of Hell. We didn't go home with each other that night. (Nearly a first, at the time, for me.) Howard and I were involved as lovers for eleven years, until his death from AIDS in 1989. I miss him so much more than I ever thought I would. Somehow we stumbled into a kind of natural, brotherly camaraderie and a love that suited both of us. Actually, I thought my life would always be like that. If not with Howard, then with someone else.

I can now say that I've definitely discovered that my expectation of an easy replacement was way off. Since Howard's death I've been involved with three different boyfriends. Each was twenty-eight when I met him. Each rumbled through a thirtieth birthday during our time together. Each was different, but each was a roller-coaster ride of a sort. All were work. None was a match made in heaven. In every case, we parted ways after two or three years—twice, rambunctiously;

once, with no hard feelings as things just gradually ended with a sigh of indifference. All three were handsome, sexy catches. But as the guidebooks say, sex isn't love. And neither, I might add, is curiosity. Or acquisitiveness. Or style.

A break in this pattern came during a New Year's Eve celebration at an ashram in upstate New York, where I was researching a book I was writing at the time. I was there to work, not to commune. With my red notebook in hand and my sensitive antennae stretched way up, I felt safe and impervious. I had a job to do. "Not like the rest of these gullible, New Age softies, concentrating on their mantras," I thought. But all the sitting and meditating finally affected even me. It was as if my insides opened up and I found myself in a cave with blue-purple lighting—a secure place where I enjoyed spending time and even became pleasantly lost. The experience wasn't totally alien. I'd been there before at different times in my life. I can remember once when I was six years old zoning out in a similar den of Ali Baba's thieves. For many years, though, I hadn't visited this alluring cave of solitude.

My forty-fifth birthday arrived a few weeks after my visit to the ashram. Soon afterward I stopped drinking, stopped smoking (the little that I had), was meditating twice a day, seeing my therapist at eight o'clock one morning and working out with my trainer at nine the next. My research on this spiritual book was leading me down a winding road that included releasing toxins at the Chopra Center for Well Being in La Jolla; reading books such as *Conversations with God*, by Neale Donald Walsch; attending a different church every Sunday. (My favorite was Saint Francis Xavier Roman Catholic church, because it had the cutest guys.)

I felt as if I had been given a shiny new deck of cards and had been told to start dealing. Secretly, I of course assumed that hidden away in this deck would be the Prince of Hearts: the boyfriend card. It was almost as if in some replay of the corny old making-a-deal-with-God scenario, I expected that if I cleaned up my act, I was going to be rewarded with a boyfriend who was successful, handsome, full of character, and, this time, with an aura of spirituality. I secretly believed that this was an unsigned, unspoken, entirely understood (by whom?) package deal. Well, the Prince of Hearts card was never played. Not even the Two of Hearts turned up. Just the opposite occurred. Every bit of sex, romance, titillation, flirting, and dating in my life went entirely flat. . . . What could be more unfair?

Something else *was* more unfair. The old solutions for finding love in all the wrong places—the consolation prizes, as it were—didn't satisfy anymore. They didn't even work when I did revert to old habits, when I was jones-ing for love, as it were. I used to be able to place imaginative ads on phone-sex lines that would immediately be answered by hot-to-trot respondents. Suddenly the special service number I kept exclusively for such anonymous admirers was not worth its $9 monthly fee. I used to be able to walk into a local leather bar and feel like Sharon Stone in her Gap T-shirt cruising into the Academy Awards. Suddenly it was as if I wasn't even there. No more eye contact. (Not drinking didn't help in diving into those fast-moving currents.) My heart just wasn't into visiting the dirty-movie theater where I had spent so many earth-opening—or so they seemed to me—evenings when I was the porn critic for a now-defunct New York City gay newspaper.

I didn't find a foxy stranger, or a boyfriend either. But I did find at that time the inspiration for this book. One evening I was downstairs—I live on the top floor of a four-story house in SoHo—at a party given by good friends and neighbors. They're a straight couple who were about to be married in June. A guest of theirs arrived with his new boyfriend. Both are film agents who live in L.A.

The new boyfriend said to me: "I've heard so much about you. I've been at so many dinners where people talked about you. How great-looking you are. What a good writer you are. What a nice guy you are. I see these little inch-by-inch photos of you in gossip columns and magazines. I'm glad to finally meet you."

"Why thank you," I answered graciously.

"But tell me, do you have a boyfriend?" he asked, leadingly.

"No."

"Well, I guess then it's all worth nothing," he responded.

"Ummmm. . . ." Long pause. "Let's not throw out the baby with the bath water. . . . What about the boyfriend within?"

"Yeah, people say things like that. But I never believe them."

His comment felt like a smack. I'm sure he was simply being unintentionally spastic. But I was challenged to try to formulate a response, to try to explain what I really meant. My first attempts, in my head of course, produced only clichés. As I replayed the scene for the third, fourth time over the next five, six weeks, though, a tingle of good feeling began percolating.

Slowly I understood more fully what I'd meant when I blurted out my quick comeback about "the boyfriend within." I was simply reaching—in a contemporary, gay way—back to an ancient idea that informs all of the traditions of wisdom with which I'm familiar, both Eastern and Western. It was the simple truth that love, happiness, and respect come from within. What we often mean when we say, "I'm looking for a boyfriend," is that we're looking for that warm feeling of happiness, or contentment, or peace and inner satisfaction, for that turning of the heart into a pond of golden nectar. Of course this sense of love, happiness, and integrity traditionally arises out of a relationship with someone else. Other people provide endless opportunities for us to extend ourselves, to reach out, to "get over ourselves." But the basic, often-mouthed-yet-still-true paradox is that we're only good at loving and being happy with others to the extent that we love and are happy being with ourselves. The Boyfriend Within is made up of our own inner qualities, considered and respected. Yet it's surprising how often such self-appreciation—as distinct from self-centeredness—is lacking.

The stranger across the crowded room is often just a mirror in which we're really seeing some of our own best qualities, the qualities of our Boyfriend Within. We project these qualities outward. We imagine that we see in the mirror of the other person someone who is going to be loving, caring, understanding, protective, stimulating, supportive, exciting; someone who will take care of us when we're down, put his arm around our shoulders during stressful periods or emergencies, and, best of all, keep us titillated and surprised and feeling sexy in the most general way all the time. What we often don't realize is that this imaginary lover is inside ourselves. And it's one of the standard mysteries of life that when we locate that tall, dark, wise, and handsome lover within ourselves, he's more likely to materialize out of that mirror and become an actual three-dimensional good guy in our lives—though always a bit less controlled and perfect than the man in the mirror. Halls of mirrors are fun for a while, but ultimately they're frustrating. Better to experience the relaxation and growing satisfaction that comes from the real thing, the Boyfriend Within. Then, even if life doesn't provide a matching fund in the form of a new beau, or a longtime companion perceived in a new light, you won't really mind so much. I promise.

As I was going to bed one night during my season of questioning, I realized this absence of contentment in myself quite strongly. I noticed that two pairs of beat-up sneakers and lots of dirty white socks were strewn next to my futon bed. The bed itself was cov-

ered with numerous sections of the Sunday *Times.*
Sheets and blankets were rolling in contradictory directions. There was a crusty cereal bowl nestled between two misshapen pillows. The alarm didn't need
to be reset since I'd overused its "snooze" option six-
teen hours earlier. The shade had snapped to the top
of the window, where it was likely to remain, only to
be cursed the next morning when the sun began to
glare.

I was prepared, as usual, to ignore the chaos. I
was about to simply roll into bed, quickly turn down
the halogen lamp, and curl into a fitful sleep, in denial about the sorry state of my cluttered room. This
time, though, I stopped myself and asked what I
would do if I had a guest sleeping over. Instantly I
knew the answer to that question. So I decided to experiment. I stuffed the dirty clothes in the hamper.
Threw away the *Times.* Made the bed. Lit my yellow
Museum of Modern Art vase-sized candle, and some
incense as well. Turned the light down to an amber
glow. Prepared a cup of warm milk sprinkled with
nutmeg and cinnamon. Put on a CD of Franz Liszt's
late piano pieces. Eventually I drifted off into a cloud
of sleep much deeper than any I would have experienced if I'd simply left the mess to take care of itself.
Perhaps without fully realizing its implications at the

time, I was now having my first date with the Boy-friend Within.

I soon realized from chatting around, though, that this nifty concept of the Boyfriend Within was vulnerable to all sorts of misinterpretation. At its joki-est it could sound like the title of a manual for one-handed entertainment. At its worst, like a sermon on the joys of narcissism and self-love, a sort of New Age revisiting of Ayn Rand on "the virtue of selfishness." It could be interpreted as adult nostalgia for the secret companion of our childhood, the imaginary friend we spoke to when our actual friends were too much trou-ble. And it, of course, brings to mind the prescription to get in touch with "the Child Within" that's already current in our culture. Put "the Child Within" together with gay romance and you end up with something that could sound like the platform of the National As-sociation for Man-Boy Love.

"The Boyfriend Within's really about taking care of the little boy inside you, right?" a friend asked. Well, yes and no. The problem with such interpreta-tions is that they tend to be pat generalizations or name brands meant to apply to everyone. As I came to discover gradually, the Boyfriend Within is made of qualities we find attractive in ourselves but often imagine others to possess more fully, as well as of dormant qualities we wish to nurture and grow. Either way, each person's cluster of qualities is unique and peculiar to them, and, like all of us, is always changing and evolving as well. The Boyfriend Within isn't some high concept, after all. He's part of yourself.

So there's more to meeting the Boyfriend Within than mere wishful thinking, or philosophizing. About a week after my initial sleepover with the Boyfriend Within, I designed a practical technique, a *Procedure* for keeping him steadily and reliably in my life. Exasperated with reading a cacophony of self-help books and trying to apply them to my particular pain, I simply sat down one day with a pad and felt-tip pen and started asking some basic questions about my life. You know the sort: Why am I sitting home alone on a sunny Sunday? Why do all my close relationships backfire? When will love come my way? But this time, I waited for the answers. Not from some channeled spirit, but from a self-reliant source of wisdom and strength within. Slowly I began to "hear" answers and to write them down. For some reason, I felt moved to write down the answers with a pen different from the one used to write the original questions—in the spirit of those gestalt psychology exercises where you switch seats to talk to different sides of yourself.

It was this Voice I "heard" that led me to get more

in touch with that part of myself I've come to think of as the Boyfriend Within. A well-known author once advised me on the subject of boyfriends: "You're the only person who knows what you really need from a lover. Don't be influenced by anyone else on this. Listen to yourself. You may be surprised." The same is true with the Voice and with the Boyfriend Within. Along the way in this book you'll be hearing some of the answers the Voice made to me. Hopefully they'll be informative. But more important, you'll be guided soon on how to use a *Procedure* with two pens and a pad of paper to get in touch with your own Voice, which could be thought of as the Voice of the Boyfriend Within, generously sharing his wisdom with you, as any good boyfriend would. I'm convinced everyone has this power. That everyone's Boyfriend Within is unique, personal. That the Boyfriend Within and the Voice go mysteriously hand in hand. (As we became more familiar, I even began thinking of the Boyfriend Within as my BFW, or Inner B.)

In the months following my forty-fifth birthday, as the curve of my romantic and sexual activity declined as precipitously as the Dow Jones in a bear market, the curve of my contacts with the Boyfriend Within began to rise. The helpful Voice gradually became an ordinary part of my life—a garden-variety voice that offered opinions on daily questions about life, love, and where to go on vacation. I didn't need communiqués from angels. I just needed to sit down and focus. I just needed a pad and pens. I was anxious to figure out some of the burning questions of my life with the newfound help of the Boyfriend Within.

I'm convinced that listening with the inner ear is a talent anyone can cultivate. Everyone has a guiding Voice within. When it is located, good results are indicated. Certainly it's made changes for the better in my life. These changes speeded up when I could locate the Voice and the Boyfriend Within as surely as I could locate the mood I think of as "The Middle of the Night"—the mood of panic about being alone, or being yesterday's news, or believing that the agent from L.A. had a point. By building a daily, casual relationship with the Boyfriend Within, I didn't escape these moods, nor did I escape true setbacks and bad times. But I began to see upsetting tremors as early warning signs, as opportunities to consult the inner compass and take direction from there. It isn't so much that my circumstances have changed, or that great fame, money, and success have come my way, but just that my attitude toward the usual stuff has been transmogrified in a completely positive way. Life with the Boyfriend Within hasn't become unrecogniz-

ably different, just smoother, warmer, and more focused and clear.

That's how this book came to be, a book I certainly never thought I'd be writing. I decided to follow
my hunch and look for the Boyfriend Within.

This is what I found.

THE PROCEDURE
FOR FINDING THE VOICE

Sit down at a table with a tablet
of paper and two felt-tip pens. I always
sit on a folding wooden chair at my
small, square kitchen table.
Whatever spot you choose,
it helps to return to the same place.

I began one day when I got
really frustrated. All the therapy and
meditating and yoga weren't enough.
And I'd had lots of the above.
I felt I had to make an effort to figure
out some questions and answers for myself.
I'd hit bottom, which you usually need to hit
before you can rise again to the surface,
and which reminds you that these problems
must finally be faced by you and you alone.
All the advice in the world won't help
unless you've found your own balance first.
My persistent pain was like an endlessly
ringing telephone. When I picked up a pen

*to jot down questions, it was like picking up the
telephone.*
All I had to do was say, Hello?
The Voice was on the other end with answers.

*At first, in the early, scattershot days, I wrote down
lots of questions.*
*I did it just to get in the mood, to get to know the
Voice,*
to hear its answers,
and to get some sense of where
we were going together. That's why two pens:
a pen for me, a pen for the Voice.
In a way, all I was doing was writing
down my most private thoughts.
But it was more than that. I know myself.
*And I know that the Voice and I are not exactly the
same.*
I wish it were me. But it's not.
I can be diffident, shy, guarded, arrogant.
The Voice is always friendly and generous.
The Voice doesn't have a shell around it.

I always felt quite good after those sessions.
I know they helped me.
This book is a record of those Q&As

and of my attempts to figure out what they meant:
It's definitely a Procedure *anyone can try at home.*
You should keep a record too. You might think of
this book as more of a compass than a map.
My answers can only point toward your own.

CHAPTER ONE

QUESTION: *Why don't I have a boyfriend?*
THE VOICE: *I don't know.*

As SUGGESTED IN the *Procedure,* for a week

or so I experimented, warming up by writing

down quick, spontaneous questions addressing

the crises of the moment—"What's wrong?" or

"How am I going to get through tonight?" or

"Should I call him back?" When I asked, for instance, how I was going to get through the night, I wrote down the Voice's response as: "Only do whatever you feel like doing. And check back with me every hour." The directive was gladly taken, and it was fun. I ended up having a late-night snack of oysters at a place down the street with a friend. I was limbering up for the dialogue and the education that was about to begin.

One day I dove in and asked one of the questions at the heart of this whole enterprise: "Why don't I have a boyfriend?" No sense wasting time, I told myself neurotically. Now, some people beginning this process already have boyfriends, and their first significant question might be different, such as, quoting the old song, "Is that all there is?" But for me, and for many others I'm sure, this boyfriend question needs to be answered and cleared up before moving on. This chapter is concerned with just that necessary clearing, a kind of romantic spring cleaning. So imagine my disappointment when I sat down in earnest to begin to reach the Boyfriend Within, only to receive the reply noted above. Needless to say, "I don't know" didn't do much for me at first, except to disappoint and really annoy.

"Humph," I thought. "Some Oracle of Delphi!

Everyone else channels all these amazing, lyrical, po-
etic, wise voices from the beyond. They get guardians
full of depth and dignity. I'm stuck with a slacker.
Next thing I know he'll be calling me 'Dude' and
shoving off on his skateboard. Just my luck." But it
was my Voice, and I was stuck with it. What do you do
when your Ouija board supplies only incoherent, gar-
bled messages? Return it?

As I delved deeper, though, I felt nudged in a direction by the vagueness of the answer. Perhaps the
Voice wasn't being so cool after all. Perhaps the Voice
was even getting warm. There may be no final explanation for those of us without boyfriends, just
guesses. We're bachelors or widowers or loners,
whether temporarily or always, whether we've been
left, or perhaps have set our standards a little too
high, or haven't been on a date in a year, or live in a
remote locale. The only exceptions are those who ab-
solutely say, "I don't want a boyfriend." And they
might not be open and flexible enough to tap into
the Boyfriend Within anyway.

The other day, while cruising the Internet, I
stopped at a cute guy's gif (graphic image) to which
he'd attached the posted caveat: "Not looking for
someone who wants to move in with me. Or who
wants to be my boyfriend. Just someone who won't be

31

able to keep his hands off me." That was simple. He doesn't have a boyfriend because he doesn't want one. (If you believe his mixed message, that is.)

A prime cause for not having a boyfriend comes from tying oneself in psychological knots. One way I know to untie these knots is with a therapist. I've been in therapy for twenty years, on and off; with an Episcopalian nun-priest-therapist, no less. I love seeing her. Where else can I talk about myself for forty-five minutes? Dwell on my every twist and turn? And not have to be polite by trading off and listening to a friend? Or be afraid that the friend I'm talking to has ulterior motives and might secretly be saying what I want to hear, or might secretly want to pull me in or push me away? It's worth the money to have a neutral spot at which to debrief every week.

A friend told me recently of the "pattern" he'd "discovered" in therapy—though it had been perfectly evident to all of us around him since day one. He was guilty of dancing the notorious "cha-cha." It goes like this: He would become involved with someone. They'd quickly become boyfriends. After a few months, he'd start to feel restless, weird, angry, trapped. He'd move a few steps one way, then twist and go in another direction. He'd cause problems. Eventually the boyfriend would split. As soon as he'd split, my friend would want him back.

He'd send roses, call, show up with passes for press seats at a Calvin Klein fashion show. This stunt was pretty transparent.

Now, through therapy, he knows why he doesn't have a boyfriend, or at least why he *might* not. And luckily he knows what he can do about the situation. With work, he can become attuned to the alarms that warn of another crisis. When they go off next time, he can find the reflex within himself to remedy the situation. That way he'll have a boyfriend in bed with him, asleep, spooning, if he wants. Not necessarily, of course. But it's possible.

Like my friend with his classic "cha-cha" routine that gets in the way of meeting, falling in love, or staying together, everyone has insecurities that may lead to patterns of conflict and avoidance. Some people feel they're basically unlovable. Or that other people are unlovable. Some are control freaks. Some are afraid of being suffocated. Some confuse sex with love. Some confuse unavailability with attractiveness. Some prefer fireworks. Some are searching for Daddy. Some are running away from Daddy. And on and on it goes. As Annie Lennox put it: "Some people like to abuse you. Some people like to be abused."

•   •   •

ALONG the way to finding the Boyfriend Within, I've found it useful, besides contacting the Voice as outlined in the *Procedure,* to also do a series of "Awareness Exercises." These are close to the sorts of exercises you might do in therapy, or in self-discovery seminars. Some are designed to make us aware of patterns of thinking, feeling, or behaving that have contributed to unhappy habits in our lives. In sixties lingo, their purpose is "consciousness raising." Others are designed to help us develop new ways to contact and stay attuned to the BFW. These exercises can be quite practical: In one case, we'll be trying to dream up as many dates as possible with our Boyfriend Within. Or they can be more theoretical: In another case, we'll be listing repercussions of looking at the world as something other than a mail-order catalog from which to pick boyfriends. If relating to the Voice and the Boyfriend Within is the heart and soul of this book, the Awareness Exercises are its muscles and skeleton. Both are necessary.

You'll need only one pen to scratch down your responses in the Awareness Exercises, and you might want to keep a record of what you write—to look back on, to add to. These responses won't be as charged or unpredictable as the guiding or oblique pronouncements from a sometimes cryptic Voice. Unlike the Q&A format for contacting the Voice, they mostly involve list making. Doing these exercises, however, helps greatly in moving the process of finding the Boyfriend Within into fast-forward. There will be fifteen Awareness Exercises spread out throughout the book—taken together, they can point you in the right direction.

Awareness Exercise One

Write down a list of your own neurotic patterns. Once written out, these bumps in the night lose some of their power to control and alarm. They become demystified. The door is off their closet, so to speak. Exorcising, as we've learned from the movies, is always about naming the demon. So you can begin to exorcise these neurotic routines by putting them into words. Once you begin, you'll find other patterns occurring to you while you're walking down the street or driving in a car. Go back and add them to the list. Every time you identify one of these neurotic patterns, your emotional IQ will shoot up about five points. Here's my own list, and a few explanatory comments:

- I seem to be attracted to villains, to the sort of guy who plays pirates in movies.

Everyone else takes one look at him and thinks, "I don't trust that guy." I look at him and think, "Hmmmmm. . . ." A related type is the "gimbo" (a gay bimbo), whose muscles and physical desirability make him an attractive arm to want to hang on, regardless of any lack of depth. Whoever these gimbos really may be, I'm drawn to their potential as cartoon characters in the self-created comic strip of my love life.

- I'm sometimes drawn to people who seem at first capable of making my life easier.

They mother me. Or, more important, they father me by having the big bucks, buying dinner and theater tickets, and always paying for the cab. They have famous and influential friends to introduce me to. The problem is that eventually there's a price to be paid. And just as with a new credit card, the bill usually doesn't come for a couple of months. That's when the demands, and the uglier parts of their character I've chosen to overlook, become more glaring. And I find myself feeling like just a glorified gigolo. (This scenario, of course, worked better circa age twenty-two.)

- After a few weeks with anyone, my eye begins to wander.

I feel I'm missing something. I want to go out, party, develop new tastes. I love romance and the excitement of getting to know someone. But after a while I begin to feel as if I'm back home living with my parents, listening to them argue, staying in at night doing homework under duress. I don't like anything that reminds me too much of the childhood blahs. As a result, I quickly reconfigure my new beau as a prison guard or truant officer or busybody.

Almost everyone can tally inner and outer explanations for their predicament in life. I've developed quite a list of my neurotic patterns by making Awareness Exercise One a part of my regular mental routine. A few days after making my original list, I suddenly noticed that I *always* give my phone number but never ask for the other guy's number in return. I'm then left feeling either rejected, all-alone-by-the-telephone style, or pursued. It's a self-imposed version of the chador worn by Islamic women. I veil my desires. My last boyfriend was perfect for my neuroses: He could only be reached by voice mail—which meant he was consistently distant, unavailable, and in control.

Of course, not everyone who doesn't have a boyfriend has such obvious neurotic patterns to blame, or to change—though to some extent we all have a few. In Awareness Exercise Two we'll be dealing with "environmental factors," which do affect everyone and which can have an impact on whether you're single or involved: age, location, death, sickness, career. (There *is* a real world out there, after all.) We can look at this situation in another context: Many people who wish to have a million dollars, don't. Is this just because they don't really want a million dollars? No, they typically have little if any control over the matter. Some live in North Korea. Some don't want to do the dirty deeds that might be required to make a million dollars, given their age and station and educational level. Some just don't have the tools. Some aren't in the right place at the right time. These are all examples of factors that are part of an environment and not entirely self-created.

I don't mean to belittle the homespun truth that anyone who really wants a mate can usually find one. Or that anyone who doesn't, whether consciously or un-, often doesn't really want one. Or to suggest that dark forces of the id aren't sometimes at work that need to be exposed and named and put to rest. But I also know that in the real world on which we stub our toe, shit happens. People grow older. There are differences in maturity: You just might not have the patience for an otherwise buff guy who continuously comes up with the-dog-ate-my-homework excuses, such as "My answering machine must have lost your message." As a friend reasonably complained, "It seems the saner I get, the fewer people there are to relate to."

AWARENESS EXERCISE TWO

Write down the environmental factors involved in your not having a boyfriend. Not having met the right person is certainly an acceptable explanation. But there are others. Most people find this second list more surprising than the first. In this psychological era we've perhaps become more used to contemplating the navel of our feelings than smelling the coffee. Both aspects of experience need to be taken into account. Here are a few examples of my own environmental factors:

- AIDS

    Certainly, among gays, this disease has been an entirely unexpected meteor crashing into everyone's best-laid plans. I've experienced the special difficulties when two people of different HIV-status become romantically involved but feel *medically* uncomfortable with each other. Disease and death are real, though. We didn't invent them.

- Career

    I hate to admit that each one of my last three books has been written mostly during a bachelor phase. I'd rather say that they flourished like flowers in the nurturing sun of love. But it's not true. Selfish spans of uncompromising hours were incalculably helpful. Remember the quite honest line in *Philadelphia,* when Tom Hanks, playing a gay lawyer, admitted, "I love the law." People can love their jobs, love success. Perhaps for them it's not the moment for romance. Give them a few years. To everything there is a season.

- Not having met the right person

    Sure, there's *someone* for everyone. But who wants just someone? Unless you want a boyfriend the way you want a Jag or a Range Rover, for image and kicks, you might want to hold out. For me, the prospect of a boyfriend has to compete with a quality of life that's already set, and at least pretty satisfactory. As in one of the worn clichés of on-line profiles on AOL: "I'm looking for Mr. Right, not Mr. Right Now."

And then there are those who simply aren't being honest with themselves. These types love to join in the complaining circle at dinner, moaning about being boyfriendless, but truth is, they just don't want a boyfriend. On an unwritten, probably unconscious ledger sheet they've already added up the pluses of a boyfriend versus the minuses. The minus column has secretly won out as the more compelling to them.

Awareness Exercise Three

List the pluses and minuses in having a boyfriend. To find out what you're really thinking, draw a line down the middle of a blank sheet of paper, listing on one side the pluses of having a boyfriend, and on the other, the minuses. See how the columns add up. One side might prove stronger than the other because of a longer list of entries, or because of the undeniable draw of a few concerns of most importance to you. Both quality and quantity need to be weighed in this decision. Maybe you'll discover the Boyfriend Within is the terminus on your particular route, the truly preferred destination. Why waste the effort pretending to look for a boyfriend if you're really ambivalent?

On the plus side, I'm attracted by the advantages of:

- Intimacy
- Division of labor
- Nursing
- Sleeping together
- Buying real estate together

On the minus side of my ledger sheet, I find that I'm certainly put off by:

- Snoring
- Having to report in
- Enduring a doubled number of obligatory parties and dinners

In my own case, the plus side wins out because of both the quality and quantity of the positive items listed.

WHETHER being single has been subconsciously chosen, or is a matter of circumstance, or has been selected with eyes clear and unblinking, I find there's often, maybe even relentlessly, a stigma in our postliberated era to not having a boyfriend. This stigma can manifest itself as a pointed finger accusing one of crimes such as an "intimacy problem!" Notice, next time, that everyone who uses such clunky terms hasn't necessarily paid the tuition, or put in the study time, to get the advanced degrees in counseling and psychology to license them to use such jargon. They're talking the talk without having walked the walk. The unfortunate, and frequent, assumption behind these comments is that people who aren't coupled are lemons, defectives, emotional squirts.

When Howard and I were having our truly screwy, though wonderful, time together, friends, especially distant ones, would look at us with dewy eyes as though we were somehow to be emulated. "If only I were you, I'd be happy," their goo-goo faces seemed to say. "If only you knew," I always thought (humorously) in return. I loved Howard. I was happy with him most days. But somehow our brand of love and happiness wasn't the item these friends' eyes told me they were in the market for. Now that I'm boyfriendless, I get lots of looks and comments that tell me just the opposite of what they said before. "I'm sorry you're a Tin Man, missing a heart," they seem to be saying. Like Judy Collins, I've looked at life from both sides now. Or, more accurately perhaps, life's looked at me from both sides now.

Pondering these matters, I gradually learned to make room for the Voice's answer: "I don't know."

There is a place, too, for my therapist's answers. And maybe there's even a place for the Hollywood agent's skepticism. But deep in the heart of the Voice's slacker reply is a nonjudgmental, haunting tone that is not only celestine and hip and trendy, but may be more respectful of the way things are, the way people are.

Recently, when I was getting a haircut, my barber said, quoting *his* therapist: "The reason you're on earth is to experience life. That's it. Everything else, including whether you get love or money, is just icing." I don't know if the Voice was exactly saying *that*. But he (why not she? why not it? I'll have to get back to that question) . . . he was saying something similar.

It's worthwhile hedging your bets, though, by continuing to work at the question of why you do what you do. Take time every day to revisit selected Awareness Exercises from this chapter and those to come. Really get in there and dig out the blackened weeds deeply rooted in your own soil. But I'd caution you that one session of self-examination a day is plenty, and remember it's for yourself and should be done alone. It's certainly not something real boyfriends need to do together—perform surgery on each other's psyches. They just need to love each other. And that's not territory you need to overdo with your Boyfriend Within, either—as you gradually begin to know him and court him and love him.

I can't believe how many times I've had this maddening "Why don't I have a boyfriend?" conversation recently. The next time you find yourself having this conversation with someone—and if you're caught reading this book, chances are you will—try taking on some of the attitude of the Voice. It's okay to say, "I don't know," because you must admit finally that you don't know everything about anyone, not even yourself. So maybe say: "I don't know why I don't have a boyfriend, and I don't know why you don't have a boyfriend. We may never know. You may someday. Or you may never. But *I* think you're boyfriend material." Or just throw civility to the winds and kiss him on the lips, or hold his hand, or touch him, or stroke his back, or at least smile . . . something. You'll probably like yourself better as a sympathetic know-nothing anyway than as a correct know-it-all. I found "I don't know" to be a useful mantra in many situations. And more often than not, truthful: "I don't know."

Incidentally, as someone who's been in boyfriend heaven, I can tell you that there comes a time when even boyfriends would do well to discover the Boyfriend Within. I watched my relationship with Howard go from loneliness to fudgy togetherness to a kind of aloneness again: that is, the two of us sitting peacefully in the same room—reading, say—but thrown back on our own resources. That's a phase of coming down to earth that other coupled friends of mine have corroborated as being their experience as well. It could be that between lovers the prescription for the Boyfriend Within might become a fandango, a recipe for a threeway, or even a fourway. Anyway, many boyfriends within and without! I'm losing count.

I think, too, about gay teenagers. I never had a huge mess of a problem with coming out. I went to Columbia College in the 1970s. Even though I hadn't had sex with a boy since my friend Bobby, when I was thirteen, I just marched down to the Gay Lounge, met the president of the gay student group, who took me to meet the dean of housing, who was also gay, and I ended up with a great room in Furnald Hall. Talk about positive reinforcement! But if I'd known about the Boyfriend Within when I was pining after the blond basketball player I had a crush on in junior high, I might have had a less miserable, if no less frustrated, adolescence. Not to mention having somewhere to go with my big secret of being gay—I did manage to keep this secret, or thought I did, all through high school. I know that many gay teenagers today still are troubled (and too many become hopeless and commit suicide). If they find their Boyfriend Within, they'll at least have someone or something to tide them over until they get out of Iowa or the Panhandle, and perhaps they'll have invaluable practice early on in the ways of adult love. They might even feel better about life and themselves.

And what about women? I hear my women friends discussing this topic even more than my gay friends—if that's possible. Certainly, with divorces on the rise, many people of all sexual persuasions are finding a new need to become acquainted with the Boyfriend/Girlfriend Within. My straight trainer hasn't had much luck looking for a Girlfriend Without after his last, who put up with him for about three years. Between dumbbell sets, I tried out a variation of the concept on him. "Maybe you should get in touch with the Girlfriend Within." I suggested. "Would that make me a lesbian?" he asked. I didn't have an answer. Though I guess the Girlfriend Within brings together straight men and lesbians in a way I hadn't considered before. They might both be looking for the Girlfriend Within. But that's just too confusing. I'm losing count again.

I think that finding the Boyfriend Within—or the Girlfriend Within—as in finding the Boyfriend Without: that real, 3-D boyfriend, can be a path toward greater realization, or what is called dharma in Buddhism. The idea of dharma, as I understand it from some popular American version of Buddhism that's been filtered down from college courses and pop-psych books and Allen Ginsberg and Hermann Hesse and Keanu Reeves in *Little Buddha,* is that you can follow a path of service, or a path of religious devotion, or a path of mental or even physical discipline, and eventually arrive wiser and happier, and at the same spot as those on other paths. The point is to choose a path and stick with it, stick with *anything* that's not hurtful. Your consistent focus may release a force that will unpack lessons along the way: different ways, same lessons. I don't know why a path of romantic love couldn't do the same. It seems so much more up the alley of everyone I know. I've been on it—with occasional detours down its sexual side-paths—for some time. And now here I am at an intersection. I can at least corroborate that there is change and growth and help and some happiness to be had on such a path. Enlightenment, though, I don't know. There it is again: *I don't know.*

AWARENESS EXERCISES:

1. List neurotic patterns that might be getting in the way of your meeting, getting to know, or learning to happily live with a boyfriend.

2. List environmental factors that may in part explain any difficulties you are experiencing in meeting, getting to know, or living with a boyfriend.

3. Draw a line down the middle of a blank sheet of paper. On one side, list the pluses of having a boyfriend. On the other side, list the minuses. See how your own personal ledger sheet balances out.

CHAPTER TWO

QUESTION: *Who is the Boyfriend Within?*

THE VOICE: *Well, in your case, he's definitely your "better half."*

By THE TIME the above exchange came about with my Voice, I'd grown used to his sarcasm. It turns out that my particular Voice has quite a sense of humor. More than I do, certainly, or at least more than I usually allow to seep into my writing. Getting acquainted with the Voice has already added something new and positive to my life. Of course, not everyone might consider sarcasm a boon. But I did. I realized that much of my problem with self-help wisdom has always been the vapid, smug, air-conditioned tone of voice in which so much of it is delivered. The contents are fine. But the package is too often a matter of Hallmark Greeting Card meets Suspiciously Blissful Cult Member. I'm glad my Voice has some bite. You may have found some refreshing, surprising qualities in your own Voice by now as well. If you haven't, be patient. You may, gradually.

Thankfully this time the Voice's answer to my query wasn't so cryptic as his "I don't know" of chapter 1. Flip, yes. Cryptic, no. I knew immediately just what he was poking at. He was poking at the burning personal issue I always associate with Romans 7:15 in the New Testament. That's where Saint Paul, sounding dangerously, at least at first blush, like a nut case, cries out: "I cannot even understand my own actions. I do not do what I want to do but what I hate." Now, Saint Paul—with his Epistle to the Romans, his other epistles, and his reputation as the man responsible for some of the favorite quotations used by self-righteous preachers when they want to put down homosexuality—has never been one of my heroes. Even Romans 7:15 could sound like a puritan argument against the desires of the flesh. And it may well be. You know the drill: Anything that feels good is bad. Anything that requires self-discipline or self-denial is good. Gays define themselves at least in part by their willingness to act on their sexuality and hormonal drives. They want satisfaction. They gotta be them and be accepted and be happy as well. Ergo gays must be bad.

Needless to say that wasn't my association when this particular verse became one of my mantras during my forty-fifth year of grasping at any seemly explanation floating by. But I did feel that I needed rewiring. My romantic life and loves had blown enough fuses in the past decade that I was beginning to wonder. I felt as if I were shorted out somehow. As if the wires of my life had been crossed, as if a white wire had been connected to a black wire, and a black wire to a white. The result was that love and romance too often became associated with bad feelings, bad choices in partners, and general emotional power outages.

Take Dirk. One morning, during week two of a liaison that went on for almost a year, we had just rolled out of bed. I was brewing coffee. Dirk, wearing my green plaid Brooks Brothers bathrobe, dialed the phone while sitting across from me on the couch. He explained without flinching to his unnamed interlocutor: "I'm in the phone booth on the train coming in from Long Island. I'll be at Penn Station in a half hour." He then strolled off nonchalantly to shower and shave. Whenever I tell this story, everyone hoots and hollers at my naïveté. Why didn't I say anything? Wasn't that a glaring tip-off that something was wrong with this picture? At the time, though, I blocked my response. Dirk rewarded my acceptance of his unusual behavior by telling me more of what I wanted to hear. "I'm the one you've been praying would come your way," he once bragged. He made claims that perhaps only a Boyfriend Within could truly satisfy—that he was going to make me happy, secure, and loved forever. In return, I spliced the white wire of my love and affection to the black wire of his evidently sociopathic personality.

A woman friend of mine, Gini, was seeing a self-made millionaire from Los Angeles who'd recently separated from his wife. He had a habit of getting off the phone in a manner that would leave her somehow terminally off the hook as well. Once he was calling from his cell phone while driving on the freeway. "I'm going through a tunnel, I'm losing you, I'll call you back at the other end," he said, his voice carried away in the gust of an electronic dust storm. He didn't call back. She actually worried that he'd been involved in an accident. She left several messages on his cell phone voice mail. No reply. In those early days, the two had no mutual friends, and she half believed that she'd lost him in some horrible pileup. When he called back ten days later, he was entirely relaxed and oblivious. "I've been in Hawaii, why?" he responded to her startled question about his whereabouts.

One Saturday night I went with my friend Mike to G, a gay bar in Manhattan's Chelsea district that looks like a Banana Republic store filled with Banana Republic–style models from their latest ad campaign. We sat next to each other on a banquette to watch the show. Nearby a cute, generically Italian-looking guy—dashing dark eyes, dark eyebrows, five o'clock shadow—sat hunkered on a hassock behind his boyfriend, who was perched in front of him. He kept one arm around his boyfriend's chest, feeling him up nonstop while beaming stares at Mike. When we began to leave, the romancer with a modular personality rubbed Mike's leg as he walked by while continuing to fondle his boyfriend's pecs. When I told another friend a few days later about this triangular incident, he said casually, "Oh, I know him." As proof, he described not only the guy but the same incident, with himself as the third point of the triangle. "Now there's a *real* man for you," he joked.

I tell these stories because they each provide examples of crossed wires, of going for drama rather than substance, of what happens when good people feel drawn to "bad news." I liked Dirk all the more because he kept me on pins and needles. Without the slings and arrows of uncertainty piercing me every so often, I would have been content to look at the two of us disappointingly sitting in my apartment without much to say to each other. With all the startling lies, I became too distracted to notice. I mistook mystery for true interest. Similarly, Gini's entrepreneur learned that he could count on her to take his calls. If she didn't, who knew when the next opportunity might come, or when the battery might go dead in his cellular phone midsentence. The gigolo at G instinctively understood the theatricality and power of unsettling triangular intrigue.

The best depiction I know of a character with just such crossed wires can be found in my favorite rental video, Alfred Hitchcock's *Vertigo,* where Jimmy Stewart plays Johnny, an ex-detective plagued with vertigo who chooses dizzying romance over reliable affection—with disastrous results. The woman drawing him into a doomed drama is Judy/Melanie, played as both ice princess and cheesy salesgirl by Kim Novak. You may remember her in high heels and couture dress, navigating madly up the right angles of the vertiginous wooden stairs of the bell tower of a Spanish mission outside San Francisco. But the character who haunts the movie—and me—is Midge (played by Barbara Bel Geddes). She's the lingerie designer who's there unconditionally for Johnny, waiting to pour his scotch, steer him to his next lead, and visit him in the sanitarium to help pick up the pieces of his life after he cracks up. Depicted as the sort of 1950s reliable good girl whom men wouldn't bother to make passes at, she's the very heart of nurturing love. And, of course, she hardly registers as a blip on Johnny's malfunctioning psychic screen.

Yet Midge seems perfect to me as my Boyfriend Within—allowing for some gender bending from central casting. For in her direction lie sanity, peace, happiness. Of course, if Johnny had gone for Midge there wouldn't have been a movie. And it's a given that we all like a little drama in our lives, and a few exciting plot twists. It's exciting to have our hot buttons pushed. But one way to describe the change that began happening in me when I got in touch with the Boyfriend Within was that I made some room in my life as well for Midge's contribution.

My purpose, though, isn't to lay my Boyfriend Within on you. You have to find your own. And everyone's has a slightly different constitution. For instance, I have friend—two male, two female—for whom creativity rather than intimacy is the Big Issue. They really do seem to have paintings and pop songs and novels and movies in preproduction within them. Yet they have a creative block about allowing themselves to do the necessary painting, or piano playing, or automatic writing that would let their particular genie out of his bottle. Three of them trace their stopped corks back to childhood repression; one dismisses such explanations as corny. In each of their cases I have a hunch that they'd find their Boyfriend Within to be quite a creative spirit. If mine is Midge, theirs may be Jackson Pollock, the abstract expressionist artist with apparently boundless energy and a savage, primitively inchoate desire to reinvent the wheel of art history.

For these friends, ignoring their Boyfriend Within is tantamount to denying their own creativity. They have trouble admitting that the little snatches of a tune that come to them in the middle of the night, or the great opening image they envision for a movie, or the urge to merge colors on a flat surface, really matter. They tend to think that such necessities of life for the creative person are really just luxuries reserved for someone else—for Michelangelo, or Wolfgang Amadeus Mozart. While my dates with the Boyfriend Within tend to be much quieter, more nurturing, and stress free than other appointments in my life, theirs could be high-energy opportunities to express themselves.

Another acquaintance has such a creative green thumb that he can turn any weed into a beanstalk. Creativity isn't his problem. He moves into a bleak studio apartment in a tenement on Avenue A and two weeks later it's been transformed into a magical pashadom. He's usually content to stay there and simply be the nice guy he is. For this poet of everyday life, though, the Big Issue is networking, selling himself, getting out of a flat job as a receptionist at Potholder, Inc., where he isn't utilizing his many talents.

My creative friend may actually be uneasy about getting in touch with the driving Tony Robbins within—the part of himself filled with all the testosterone required to do business in pushy America. I think of Tony Robbins because of his late-night infomercials promising money, success, and happiness for the price of a set of his *Personal Power* audiotapes about channeling positive thinking into positive results. While the medium in which he peps us up with his big hair and big teeth might be off-putting to some, his message of the virtues of pursuing personal happiness is as old and as exhilarating as the Declaration of Independence. For my friend on Avenue A, his dates with his Boyfriend Within might be filled with making lists to focus his ambition and plot the steps: a five-month plan, a five-year plan, a fifty-year mission statement. His Boyfriend Within may actually resemble one of those moguls photographed by Annie Leibovitz for *Vanity Fair* at the annual Allen & Co. summer retreat in Sun Valley, Idaho: all tan, all business, all drive.

Whether your Boyfriend Within is more Midge or Jackson Pollock, or Tony Robbins, though, you can be sure of one thing: He's also part you. He's your chance to become more comfortable with uncharted territory that's been inside you all along. He's there to help you rewire yourself. Of course, rewiring can be an intense activity. That's why I usually only spend somewhere between a half hour and two hours at a stretch with my Boyfriend Within, engaging in some of the activities I'll be discussing in the next chapter. But during that time I get a chance to be in a relationship that doesn't involve head games, or self-destructive fantasies, or pins and needles. These are trial runs with health and happiness, or creativity and power, or peace and love. Who knows? With practice, a half hour with your Boyfriend Within today might develop into an hour tomorrow.

LOOKING for the Boyfriend Within begins much like looking for a Boyfriend Without—that real boyfriend somewhere out there in the world. There's a certain amount of taking stock that transpires. I remember reading a book I picked up at someone's summer house. Its title was *How to Marry the Man of Your Choice.* Its middle-aged author presented her dates as job interviews. She'd ask pointed questions of these prospective partners, questions designed to x-ray their character. She'd distinguish the different signals and clues dropped by these men that would point her toward her final decision. When she found a man who closely matched the blueprint of desire in her head, she'd design an agenda to move him toward a ride-into-the-sunset conclusion. Her book jacket contained a piece of information more powerful than any blurb: She'd married the man of her choice and was happy.

The persona of this author made me uncomfortable, though. She seemed a consciousness-raised revamping of the old archetype of the wily, seductive, entrapping female. I wondered if she'd ever found *her* Boyfriend Within. Yet her businesslike approach to matters of the heart did appeal to me. In searching for a closer relationship with my Boyfriend Within, I've certainly had to do a lot of analyzing, temperature taking, and list making as well. Love—whether inner or outer—seems to go hand in hand with work.

When I begin thinking about my Boyfriend Within, I always recognize first that I'm really caught somewhere between the lure of the shopping mall of boyfriend hunting and my own inner tugs toward peace and contentment, the realm of the Boyfriend Within. That is, I'm oriented at least as much outwardly as inwardly. I resist a bit. One amusing way to try to ease into a true encounter with the Boyfriend Within is not to resist at all but to give in briefly to the savor of thinking romantically—by seeing ourselves as a player in the world, or as a contestant on *The Dating Game*. If we're spirits, we're spirits in bodies, or, as Sting put it, "spirits in a material world." I promise it's only a half step from here to slipping under the wave and becoming one with your rewarding Boyfriend Within.

The next Awareness Exercise will allow us to take a cool look at ourselves as "packages"—to go on an imaginary date with ourselves and size ourselves up.

People usually come away from this exercise happier than you might expect. They're not necessarily left feeling entirely objectified at all. Often they're surprised at how much they have to offer even in the most superficial of ways: pretty face, good bod, cool clothes.

Awareness Exercise Four

Write down what might make you desirable as a companion on the open market of dating and romance. You don't even have to look at yourself with any particular sensitivity, education, insight, or moral compass. When we look at ourselves through the cocked, calibrating eyes of someone slightly less sensitive and evolved than we assume ourselves to be, what do we see? Make a list of the most attractive qualities of the "package" that is you.

Looking for the positive from the point of view of an interested party, you might be surprised at all of the pluses you'd forgotten you had, of all the wrapped gifts lying under your particular tree. Everyone has something to offer. If you don't succeed in identifying your selling points at first, keep trying. It's a cheap level of self-awareness we're going for here. If nothing else, this exercise will get you used to accentuating the positive, and the Boyfriend Within will be nothing if not positive. Among the pleasures I found I could offer at least by proxy to my imaginary appraiser were:

- A buff, toned body

    I've been going to the gym ever since I was in college. I am not now nor have I ever been a physique magazine model. But I see my trainer twice a week. I swim fifteen laps twice a week. I ride the StairMaster for forty-five minutes while catching up on the week's magazines. When matters had grown too blubbery, I did what the mirror told me and went on a diet of 1500 calories a day for a couple of months. I blush to admit it, but now I could imagine going to bed with myself—at least for the sleeping part.

- My SoHo apartment

    For ten years I lived in Hell's Kitchen in Manhattan in an apartment that looked like a cross between an eternal graduate student's and a hustler's pad. "I feel like I should leave money on the kitchen table when I walk out," one friend said snidely. Then my current apartment on the top floor of an 1839 townhouse became available. The floor planks are wide. The back windows look out on tall trees. A fireplace is a welcome fixture, even if it doesn't work. "Nice apartment," people usually say when they stop by. I'd never heard that comment during my entire ten years in Hell's Kitchen. This apartment feels as atmospheric as Thoreau's cabin. Anyone who hangs out with me at home gets to spend time in my poetic cabin as well.

- A career

The state university where I teach was generous enough to grant me tenure, and I use their Olympic-size swimming pool regularly. I've published books, magazine articles, and I'm writing a screenplay. These projects give me extra pocket money for going out to dinner, buying a Valentino suit, or taking weekend trips to inns in Vermont during leaf-peeping season. There's a feeling of accomplishment that any buddies of mine can share without even having to do the work. I've already done that part.

I've tested this Awareness Exercise on willing friends, asking for their claims to winning-contestant status. Mysteriously topping one friend's list was "my washer and dryer." Another bragged of his "extensive CD collection." A third made reference to his sexual prowess. "Blond" came up. Someone did complain, however: "I had to stop," he e-mailed me. "It was actually a strange reaction I had—as if I really didn't want to see myself objectively. Not so much because I was afraid of what I'd discover as the fact that if you never have a really clear handle on it, you can still fudge so much. . . . Verrry interesting."

The antidote to my friend's anxiety and frazzle can come from the Boyfriend Within. Just as any uneasy feelings brought up by doing the fourth Awareness Exercise can be alleviated by moving on to the fifth, designed to put us in touch with our inner qualities rather than trying to put a price tag on what we feel to be so obviously priceless. Hold onto any sensations of relief, or settling, or increased seriousness and maturity you might experience in passing between these exercises. For these are the very qualities of spirit you will be nurturing in yourself by turning further and further within.

Awareness Exercise Five

Now take a deep breath and make a list of your own most attractive inner qualities. You can replace the crass bruiser looking for a one-night stand projected in the last Awareness Exercise with someone who really cares about you, someone with depth and character.

Try to gauge which of your own personality traits would be most appealing to such a mature and discerning type. You won't discover the Boyfriend Within by doing Awareness Exercise Four. But in now writing down with clear-eyed honesty your own most attractive inner qualities, you're beginning to describe your Boyfriend Within. You're getting to know him.

This Awareness Exercise is perhaps the most valuable in the entire book. For here you actually meet your Boyfriend Within for the first time. It's like that first glimpse of a special someone across a crowded room. Some have reported seeing a glow around a stranger who went on to become special in their lives. Others can remember exactly what he was wearing, or what song was playing on the jukebox. There's the old cliché about hearing bells. Mostly, though, the importance of a new friend only becomes apparent over time, and we retrospectively color the original event to fit later events. Either way, you have to begin somewhere.

In doing this exercise, I created a longer list than usual, and one that built gradually over time. Perhaps I have a particularly healthy ego. When I asked my mother once why I was an only child, she lied, obviously, and said, "Because you were so perfect, we didn't want to push our luck." I believed her lie, and the remark forever colored my self-image, for better or worse. I think, though, that everyone can eventually come up with a list of their own positive inner qualities—those attributes that would attract them to themselves in the best of all possible circumstances. My list was:

- Sensitivity
- Self-esteem
- Sophistication
- Playfulness
- Focus
- Honesty

I don't need to spell out exhaustively the evidence I found for each of these, or all of their meanings peculiar to myself. Writing down one abstract word might not seem like much, but the words resonate with feelings that we want to grow and to live with more consistently. In Awareness Exercise Four, I derived pleasure from noticing that my developed shoulders were as sturdy as a wooden coat hanger. But I derived even more pleasure from Exercise Five by feeling the settled quality of "self-esteem," or the clear uprightness of "honesty," or the sober early-morning awakening of "focus."

This list is definitely important enough to spend some time with—both in the making and in the expanding. You might begin, as I did, with five or six characteristics, but you should continue to add to the list as you recognize more and more of these qualities within. Write them on a card small enough to fit in your wallet or pocket. Look at the card every so often. Add to it. The more familiar you become with spotting these qualities, the more familiar you become with your Boyfriend Within. You're strengthening him.

Awareness Exercise Six

For those who wish to go even further, though, there's this sixth Awareness Exercise, where you begin to write down those qualities you'd *like* to develop in the Boyfriend Within that perhaps are still dormant, faint, wishful. The divergence in different people's lists—as in different people—becomes obvious at this juncture. My list for Awareness Exercise Five constituted a fine compilation of attractive qualities. Some people shared, or might wish they shared, a few of these. But others' lists were filled with other qualities. Some I never thought about and don't particularly covet. ("Modesty," for instance, shows up on some people's lists, but not on mine.) But a few of the qualities of other people's Boyfriends Within I would very much like to have. In this case, though, you don't have to go cruising for someone new as a salve for your frustration or disappointment. You don't have to wish someone else's estimable boyfriend was yours. He's yours for the creating.

Write down those qualities you wish to develop in your Boyfriend Within. Be a genetic scientist. Think how you could rewrite the DNA code of your Boyfriend Within. My own wish list includes:

- Flexibility
- Emotional Expressiveness
- Warmth
- Generosity
- Loyalty
- Listening

By placing the two lists side by side, I could immediately see that my Boyfriend Within was more developed in areas of mind and character (sophistication, focus), and less developed in heart and soul (emotional expressiveness, generosity). By having devised my wish list of attributes I desired in my BFW, and underlining with emphasis my desire for a little

70

more warmth and human kindness from him, I began to feel results. It was Pavlovian in a way, but this time I was both the dinner bell and the salivating dog.

When finished, copy down your list of inner qualities still in development on the flip side of the card filled with the list of qualities you already possess. Memorize both; refer to them. Some Post-its, with reminders such as "Flexibility," "Listening," "Discipline," or "Positive Thinking," could be helpful if stuck in key spots—on the refrigerator, next to the phone. Recognize as well all the incidents life will send your way to test these qualities. If you're nurturing generosity, you might not whisk by the guy holding open the post office door for you as he extends a paper cup for loose change. If it's listening you're trying to cultivate, you might notice the next time your mind wanders when your best friend is discussing a crucial career move he's contemplating.

I REMEMBER the Buddha being quoted as saying something to the effect that, "The hardest thing for human beings to give up is their suffering." I think that's true. We're attached to the causes of our suffering like kids to video games. We can't get enough. We invent new and better ways to suffer all the time—in

71

sex, in work, in friendships, through technology. Learning to stop loving the bomb is a tall order and beyond my scope or that of this book. But by learning to rest awhile with the Boyfriend Within, we're actually viscerally giving up suffering for however long our sessions last. The hardest thing is weirdly among the simplest to pull off, at least for a few minutes at a time. As the poet Frank O'Hara put it: "Happiness / the least and best of human attainments." Luckily this happiness is gradually addicting.

AWARENESS EXERCISES:

4. List the most attractive qualities of the "package" that is you.
5. List your most attractive inner qualities.
6. List those qualities you want to more fully develop in your Boyfriend Within.

CHAPTER THREE

QUESTION: *How do I get to know the Boyfriend Within?*

THE VOICE: *To get to know the Boyfriend Within, you have to get outside yourself.*

INSTEAD OF ASKING and answering lots of introspective questions in this chapter, we'll be concentrating on the simple task of learning to date the Boyfriend Within. The chapter will consist of one extended and extensive Awareness Exercise—Awareness Exercise Seven. It's all about going "out" with your Boyfriend Within, the possibilities for which are limited only by your imagination and the desires and needs of your Boyfriend Within. Admittedly, though, this notion of dating takes some getting used to.

When planning dates with the Boyfriend Within, I always begin by sitting down to consider the possibilities. Do I feel like going to the movies? Eating in? Taking a walk? Going shopping? The point is that you need to schedule time with your Boyfriend Within just as consciously and intently as you would with a Boyfriend Without, or a business associate, or a new infatuation, or a cousin visiting from out of town. In this case, however, you won't need to compromise. So there will be no excuses for not having a pleasant time. You're free to do exactly what you feel like doing at the moment. And you're free to change plans on a dime. Just be careful not to cancel too often, or your Boyfriend Within might feel taken for granted or less important than any passing stranger.

I had a funny conversation recently with a friend on the topic of inner dates. He asked (sarcastically?) what kind of music my Boyfriend Within liked to listen to when we got together. I told him about some early twentieth-century French piano music we appreciated, and a Vivaldi "Gloria." "So he doesn't like the headbanger stuff?" my friend asked, knowingly referring to my occasional penchant for listening to English punk-rock bands or Satanic heavy metal when I'm in a regressive, adolescent mood. "No, he seems to like the softer stuff." Our Boyfriends Within can make some surprising mood shifts—even more than most people. But since mine is mostly designed in the nurturing Midge mode, he tends to lean pretty consistently toward the softer side of my CD rack. Less strobe, more candlelight.

Many detailed decisions present themselves when you're beginning to plot dates with your Boyfriend Within. Yet even more important than the details is the single issue brought up by the Voice in his answer: "Get outside yourself." His mystical-sounding advice is indeed key to the entire enterprise. I believe that what my own personal guru is pointing to here is the truth that getting to know a Boyfriend Within is not just a matter of thinking certain thoughts, or feeling certain feelings, or being in a certain mood. There's more involved than our whims, or wishes, or even willpower. The Boyfriend Within is not just an inspirational message. He's not merely bumper-sticker material. He's real.

The saving grace of a "real" friend or significant other, or even an annoying leech of a dubious companion, is that they can take us outside ourselves, occasionally even forcibly drag us outside ourselves. I might be in a funk, but he or she is determined to go to the movies—as I *promised*. Or one evening I'm feeling jet-lagged from a hard day at work and just want to nestle in front of the TV and watch an A&E biography of Jackie O, but a friend has made reservations at a trendy French restaurant with a stiff reservations policy. So I go, unwillingly, only to be introduced to a software company's representative who wants to send me to India to dispatch reports home for their new online travel magazine. The point is that other people can draw us out of ourselves, sometimes with beneficial results.

I assume that my Voice was implying in his answer that a relationship with the Boyfriend Within has some of these same characteristics. That is, he's not just a thought away, summoned up at a moment's notice. You need to approach him more as a commitment requiring some planning, energy, and verve, and less as a lovely pearl for meditation and contemplation. And you need to pursue activities with him in real time and space or, just as with any other relationship, he'll soon become more of a theoretical cipher than an actual option. Prove you care by making room for him in your everyday life.

If you think too much about the Boyfriend Within without taking action or making a date with him, the concept can begin to scatter in a complicated maze of contradictions. Overthinking can lead to paralysis and doubt, to simply getting lost. But the same is true with a Boyfriend Without. If you're serious about someone and are away from that person for a while, you sometimes find disquieting questions presenting themselves, questions that increase in power as they tap into your own paranoia and suspicion: Is this the right person for me? What's wrong with him? Why did he say that? Why is he so distant? Why do I put up with his endless talking about himself? Why doesn't my colleague like him? Does he see something I don't see? Then, with your head still filled with these doubts, the two of you get together for dinner at a new Korean restaurant and—poof!—the questions disappear in the reality of his actual smiling face.

Life with a Boyfriend Within can be filled with distrustful doubts and questions too. The notion that you have a "higher self" or "better half" just waiting to be cultivated and listened to makes sense. That true happiness and satisfaction come from within rather than without has ancient authority. The applicability of these truths to gay men involved in dizzying and sometimes self-destructive or inappropriately adolescent searches for boyfriends as the final solution to a lack of self-esteem is not such a stretch. We can grasp that. But nevertheless the very concept of a Boyfriend Within sometimes becomes a riddle. You can't quite wrap your head around it. And its more comic implications—unseemly narcissism, for instance—take over, undermining whatever benefit could have been salvaged, collapsing the self-help superstructure in an eruption of internal giggles and sneers.

All of these questions and doubts are natural. Have them. I do. But the Voice points to eventually moving beyond such questions. To remain quizzical is to stay paranoid, or paralyzed, or merely cynical. To go beyond the questioning phase requires time and space. It requires actually going on a date with the Boyfriend Within. It requires being in touch with the real thing. So ask the questions, even return to them, but every now and then give yourself a chance to jettison them as well.

In the rest of this chapter I'll be sharing some of my specific experiences and those of my friends in moving past these early doubts and misgivings by actually beginning to date the Boyfriend Within. You might gather some ideas here for your own dates—just as you might clip a recipe for a lamb-and-leek casserole from *The New York Times*. I'm sure, though, that your Boyfriend Within will have his own suggestions, as well as a few of his own ingredients to throw into the pot.

An Evening at Home with the Boyfriend Within

The first official date I went on with my Boyfriend Within was a Sunday evening dinner at home. It had been a long time since I'd cooked for anyone. I'd long ago come to depend on ordering take-out Chinese food, or a cheeseburger and Coke from the diner down the street. When people asked if I cooked, my habitual reply was, "I heat." The only dish I'd prepared for myself in the previous six months was couscous: add boiling water, let sit five minutes. Sometimes the five minutes could be shaved down to three or four: add canned tomatoes, canned tuna fish, then wolf down the concoction in front of the evening news. "Why bother? I'm just eating by myself" was my half-heard inner excuse.

The attraction of such hasty semiconscious dinners was that I didn't have to do much preparatory work. My date with my Boyfriend Within, however, took two hours of preparation. A neighbor advised me to go to a nearby gourmet shop and choose some prepared foods from the counter: a whole chicken, red

beets, brown rice, and cranberry juice. Then on to the
Korean deli to buy purple-and-gold arrow-shaped
flowers (I never did find out their name) and cream-
colored candles. Home to vacuum and straighten up;
set out a plate, silverware, and a glass; and return
phone calls in order to clear the slate of my answering
machine.

During dinner I keyed in a selection of Philip
Glass minimalist piano music. For a change, I concen-
trated on what I was eating. (Watching TV with the
Boyfriend Within is okay when you're advanced
enough, but in early dates it's best to get to know each
other in quieter circumstances.) After dinner I loafed
on a divan in the living room, listening to the Princess
Di funeral CD—especially perking up for John
Tavener's haunting, weirdly flat "Alleluia" at the end—
while "together" we glanced interestedly through the
Sunday *Times*.

The afterglow remained for some time. Somehow
all of my couscous dinners in front of CNN—faced too
often with the scary pumpkin of Saddam Hussein's
face—blended into one fitful dinner. The memory of
them is certainly not particularly nourishing and is often tinged with anxiety. The memory of my dinner
with the Boyfriend Within, however, has a glow about
it. I'm proud of our first evening together. The food we

ate somehow turned into a feeling that lasted. Crucial to its power is the message of self-nurturing I was sending to myself, a version of "Whose life is it anyway?" It's a potent benefit delivered much more dependably and lastingly in an action rather than in a mere thought.

The residual effects, too, were quite positive. One of the arguments for funding NASA has been that so many of the discoveries made by indulging in the luxury of space travel are actually applicable on earth—from Tang to thermostats to special cameras to new synthetic fabrics. Likewise my date with the Boyfriend Within turned out to have extra benefits. For the rest of the week I had substantial leftovers in my refrigerator—there had been no such thing as leftover couscous. My floors were dust free. I had candles to light whenever the mood struck.

Taking a Walk with the Boyfriend Within

The poet William Carlos Williams wrote that "most of / the beauties of travel are due to / the strange hours we keep to see them." Well, the beauties of taking a walk with the Boyfriend Within aren't so much due to strange hours. You don't have to get up at dawn; a midnight stroll is a choice, not a requirement. The beauty comes more from a subtle shift of approach.

When I went for my first walk with my Boyfriend Within, I headed to Greenwich Village, a part of town I'd once lived in and thought I knew reasonably well. The entire expedition lasted about an hour and a half. My walk took place on a wintry Saturday as an even light illuminated the neighborhood's nineteenth-century townhouses so they looked as if they belonged in Boston or even Amsterdam. The sky was Parisian—blustery gray blue. I stopped to read all the historical plaques—urban learning aids my Boyfriend Within was drawn to, but which I'd never really noticed before and certainly had never stopped for. I realized that on all my previous walks I'd been on my way somewhere, or had been busily talking with someone. I'd never given myself a chance to see my own neighborhood as might a visitor who'd traveled half a world just to look—dead-on, rather than peripherally.

I made one stop: at a coffee shop. I ordered a Colombian coffee with skim milk. Sat on a stool at a counter to read the complimentary *Times*. That's when I realized that my Boyfriend Within had a strong attraction not only to historical plaques but also to *The New York Times*, much stronger than my own, on my own. I realized then that perhaps a good gift for him for Christmas might be a subscription to the *Times*. (Buying a Christmas gift, birthday gift, even Valentine's gift for the BFW is one of the concepts that will begin to make sense as you advance in your relationship.)

I did feel loneliness sneak up on me every so often, though, as I turned a blank corner, or passed a couple of guys holding hands on a busier thoroughfare. Mostly these sorts of problematic responses are matters for consideration in the next chapter, on "problems with the Boyfriend Within." But I did realize that my fleeting loneliness was: (1) there, and so a feeling to be reckoned with; (2) proof that there is more to life than the Boyfriend Within, as wonderful and overlooked as he may be; and (3) a feeling often plastered over in our rush for the company of others. A walk with the Boyfriend Within—as with any thoughtful companion—can lead as serendipitously to helpful insights, self-knowledge, and so to natural growth, as to a destination successfully hiked to on an arbitrarily chosen map.

Shopping with the Boyfriend Within

Hanging out with the Boyfriend Within can be an opportunity to try new things, sprout new behavior. Like a classic, old-fashioned guy, I've never really liked to shop. Actually I didn't just dislike shopping, I froze or became numb at the concept. I'd be the one left staring into a mound of cotton sweaters—myopic, tense, and lost—while whomever I was with tabulated finds, wished-for gifts, and bargains. A married friend who suffered from the same autistic impulse told me of regularly escaping to smoke five cigarettes while his wife remained inside with a salesman, picking out clothes for him. I had previously either shopped with an expert or relied on hand-me-down's or, when most fortunate, received gifts from designers.

Luckily I live in a popular shopping neighborhood, so I simply turned the corner and started there. First I hit the new Marc Jacobs boutique where I'd seen a black cashmere coat I'd been too neurotic to buy when I'd eyed the thing a few weeks earlier. The store was minimal, stark. And the coat was gone. But as beginner's luck would have it, at the next stop—J. Crew— hung a different black wool-and-cashmere coat. I fingered it, checked out the price tag. (J. Crew was the site of an earlier botched purchase during the summer, when a coat I'd admired wasn't there two weeks later when I finally tapped the strength to return to buy it.)

A seductive salesguy with dreadlocks walked up immediately.

"That's a great coat. We only have four left. You can wear it with anything." His copper eyes were the color of his hair.

So I tried on a medium. "Do you think I need the larger size?" I asked. (A question I'd never been lucid enough to ask before.) He encouraged me toward the large. I stood staring happily into the mirror at a coat that was the male version in black wool of something, cutwise, Jane Jetson might have worn.

"I might as well just go ahead and buy it, then," I said to him, feeling the hard edges of my Amex card in the pocket of my black jeans.

I did receive a rush from that purchase. And was pumped to go on to other stores: Kenneth Cole, Armani, Gap, Banana Republic. I didn't buy anything else, just scanned for information and ideas. But I'd learned some important lessons in shopping—especially the importance of timing, of being prepared for that moment when the intersection of shopper and item add up to an emotional event.

Of course shopping, like the Boyfriend Within, has different meanings for different people. I had a friend whose mother's advice whenever he was feeling unappreciated by the world was, "Go shopping, dear. It'll make you feel better." Since he felt the world owed him a living anyway, her advice only enabled his addiction. His Boyfriend Within might well be asking for a different kind of expedition—like going to Goodwill to donate clothes, perhaps. At least on some of these outings, choose an activity you've historically found challenging—not boring, certainly, but slightly daunting. Your Boyfriend Within may show you a new way through it.

Going to Restaurants, Movies, Museums, Galleries, Ball Games

To go to public events with your Boyfriend Within is yet another step. And one you don't need to force yourself to take. One confidante asked me if I were going to go to a restaurant with my Boyfriend Within. It seemed to be a favorite activity of his. "I'm uncomfortable in restaurants by myself," I answered. "If I'm by myself, I'd rather eat at home." "But you have to," he insisted. "That's the whole point. That you don't care. That you're really not alone; you have the Boyfriend Within."

Well, as my unusually enlightened high school gym teacher used to say when we'd run laps, "You're not trying to set any world records here." Having a Boyfriend Within is not about proving anything to anybody—least of all, yourself. Let the rest of your life

be a competition, a trial, an event, a dare if you like—
but not this part. Of course if you have the sort of
Boyfriend Within who requires adrenaline and new
challenges to add briskness to an otherwise dull exis-
tence, then by all means go for it. But with Midge as
my Inner B, I'm certainly much more prone to let it
be. I never force. I do respond, though, to an inner tingle, a half-felt wish. (It's true, too, that many restaurants, including four-star ones, are now featuring
"communal tables" or serving dinner for one at areas
near the bar where you can eat alone without feeling
like a social outcast and perhaps even strike up a casual conversation with a stranger. Or bring along a
book you've been meaning to read.)

Going on public dates with my Boyfriend Within
is most often about catching up. I have lots of ac-
quaintances, and they expend themselves in lots of
different activities. When I'd hear about some of their
adventures, I'd wish I'd been there too. But usually, if I
couldn't find anyone to go along with me, I would just
let the ambition slide: "I have enough work to do at
home," I'd tell myself. The Boyfriend Within is the
perfect companion to get you out of the apartment
and to accompany you on these outings. In one weekend with the BFW, for instance, I caught an Egon
Schiele exhibition at the Museum of Modern Art,

viewed a documentary about Tibetan medicine, and attended a Golden Gloves boxing match. (My inconsistent Boyfriend Within apparently feels, like Walt Whitman, "I am large, I contain multitudes.")

With your Boyfriend Within it's possible to lead not only a double life, but a fuller life. A great addition to my life, thanks to these dates, is taking in a movie in the middle of the afternoon. Somehow I'd missed this guilty pleasure. Now I indulge regularly. It's a heightened event where the Coke tastes better, and the popcorn too. And it is indeed a case where the "strange hours" kept do add to the beauty of the experience; you can painlessly slip in to see a popular movie that you'd ordinarily need to reserve for by calling 777-FILM for advance tickets, and still you'd wait in line for a half hour to jockey for a decent seat. At noon on Wednesday it's just you, on the aisle, along with a few senior citizens. For this practical luxury, and for the adolescent pleasure of sitting in a darkened movie theater, playing hooky from 9 to 5 adult life, I'm truly grateful. And my squeamishness about tables for one in crowded restaurants definitely doesn't apply to an equally guilty lunch of a Big Mac in the kiddie-colored burger palace a half hour before show time.

"Sure, the lunch counter at Burger Heaven or a

corner table at MacDonald's is safe," a more adventur-
ous friend with a thrill-seeking Inner B protested
when I bragged about my solitary burger. "But what
about a fancier spot?" He put this notion to the test by
going solo to Le Madri, a tie-and-jacket-style northern
Italian restaurant in Chelsea. His lunchtime outing
was a success, and he had a pleasant enough time,
though admitted to removing his glasses to be surrounded by a blur of color and activity without actually feeling the need to participate. "Reality only
intervened when the waiter entered my tiny realm of
vision," he confessed.

Yoga, the Gym, and other Sensual Pleasures with the Boyfriend Within

Talking or even thinking about getting physical with
the Boyfriend Within requires some subtle balancing
and tact. Neuroscientists have been presenting a lot of
evidence lately that the supposed distinction between
mind and body, or thoughts and feelings, is false.
We're really a unified field of energy manifested in different ways, it seems. Yet this philosophical and scien-
tific development doesn't mean that people don't
sometimes *feel* that the body is better left out of discussions of emotional happiness. Blame it on the puri-

tans, I guess. They're always an easy target. But whoever we blame or don't blame, the reality is that getting to know your Boyfriend Within can be as much a physical experience as it is mental, psychological, and emotional.

My favorite physical date with the Boyfriend Within has always been yoga class. My favorite instructor is a young woman with a short pageboy haircut who ends each class with a meditation on following our hearts throughout the week. Her prayerful thought is accompanied by a gesture (or "mudra") of the fingers of our hands pressed together while pointing outward like spokes of a wheel. But the hour and a half before is taken up mostly with stretches, bends, breathing exercises, lunges, squats, twists, turns, and pushes and pulls that uncover creaks and tight spots in my body I never knew were there. Yoga shines an inner light on those hard-to-get-to places. When I leave I feel more flexible, lighter. As the Boyfriend Within is identified with a "higher self," he's also identified with a toned and tuned-up body.

The gym works too. In *What Really Matters: Searching for Wisdom in America,* Tony Schwartz went on a pilgrimage, experimenting with everything from the Human Potential Movement to biofeedback to enneagrams and est. But he wound up being the most straightforwardly positive about weight training as a path to "wisdom," or at least to health and well-being. I've certainly found the aftereffects of working out to be well worth the hour spent, whether due to endorphins, sweat, or the confidence that comes from a cosmetic lift. I usually work with a trainer when weights are involved—I'm still worried they'll crash on my head, or that I'll lunge down and never straighten up again. When I'm working out alone with the Boyfriend Within, however, I tend to aerobics, especially to climbing a stairway to health on the StairMaster, either concentrating on my breathing, or flipping through the week's selection of glossy magazines. One of the mysteries of the gym is the way in which physical exertion can turn thoughts around, reframing a day and opening access to that clearer and more serene atmosphere in which my own BFW thrives.

How the body came to be grounds for deprivation and mortification in popular religions of both the East and West is a matter for scholars of religion. Certainly America has an odd double standard. Sexuality is presented both as the grail of emotional release and fulfillment and as a scarlet, X-rated source of all pain and retribution. The prevalence of sex jokes is just one indicator of the nervous hilarity that surrounds the subject. As I've said, whenever I would talk about the concept for this book, a common reaction was the masturbation joke: "Is it a one-handed manual?"

Whether solo orgasms are part of your relationship with your Boyfriend Within is actually less important than it apparently seems. The outcome falls under the six-of-one, half-dozen-of-the-other category of discernment. What is important is involving your body in your developing awareness of yourself as you expand your relationship with the Boyfriend Within. And not relying invariably on the quick fixes: a video popped into the VCR, an edgy magazine retrieved from under the bed, a stop at the *Playboy* channel. Like quick dinners eaten in front of the TV, or tumbling into an unmade bed surrounded by yesterday's news, the resulting feeling can be as much of stress or distraction as of stimulation and satisfaction. In all these cases, the pleasure of the process is lost in the handy dispensing of the result.

By spending casual time in the bathtub, or on the bed, with the Boyfriend Within, you have the possibility of opening up to a new and richer relationship with your own body. One of the great pluses of getting to know a Boyfriend Within is trying out new behavior, or new approaches to old behavior. Cultivating the garden of your own body, as it were, without the requirements of satisfying someone else or too automatically satisfying yourself, you can begin to explore rhythms and unfettered feelings previously unknown. You can learn the often overlooked thrill and tingle of being in touch with what is no less than Love's body. Few self-gifts are greater, or more steeped in the element of pure pleasure.

As the nature of everyone's Boyfriend Within varies, so naturally do their dates with him. I mentioned in the last chapter that my Boyfriend Within was a Midge type. And so a lot of my dates with him involve relaxing, nurturing activities—dinners at home, yoga, oils and incense. For those whose model is closer to the Jackson Pollock creative Boyfriend Within, their dates might tend more toward getting out canvas and paint, taking a dance class, composing a tune on an electronic keyboard. Or for the thrill-seeking Tony Robbins model, there's always skydiving, mountain climbing, or networking at a local alumni club. One person's date might be another person's job, or snooze.

Don't be afraid to try out a lot of different date concepts. Some will work; some won't. Since my chicken-and-red-beet-dinners from the gourmet shop have become weekly affairs, my diet has been greatly enhanced. As for boxing matches, though, I've left those and other sporting events to group outings. You too will probably find that every date won't be successful for you and your Boyfriend Within. If you find yourself feeling excessively lonely, or bored, that's a bad sign. But gradually you'll find yourself doing a regular "Sunday thing" more often. Or gradually you'll become an expert on movies, or you'll be reading the newspaper every day, or you'll have completed your first one-act play. (Creative dates tend to be among the most popular with many in my immediate circle.)

Just remember to be honest and true to yourself in the dates you choose. This is definitely a case where you'll be getting what you wished for. Like longtime couples, or pet lovers and their dogs, you may find yourself, as time goes on, looking more and more like your Boyfriend Within.

Awareness Exercise:

7. Plan and go on dates with your Boyfriend
    Within.

CHAPTER FOUR

QUESTION: *What if I'm having problems with my Boyfriend Within?*

THE VOICE: *You have to meet the Boyfriend Within where he lives, on his own turf.*

EVENTUALLY EVERYBODY SINGS the

blues. There's no getting around it. Indeed, all

those rows of self-help books wouldn't be on

the shelves if readers weren't trying to deal

with, among other things, their own blues: the

kind that seem to sneak up out of nowhere, then sink back again into nothingness, usually unnamed and misunderstood. The great accomplishment of a singer like Billie Holiday was to instill in words and music an emotion that, coupled with the mature beauty of her voice, made a paradox of a great blues song such as "Ain't Nobody's Business If I Do"—a song essentially about a very unbeautiful subject, spousal abuse: "I swear I won't call no copper / If I'm beat up by my poppa." She transmogrifies, even transcends the feeling by dealing with it artistically.

Negative feelings and actions are dross that *can* be turned into gold with a little art or alchemy. In this chapter I'll be talking about those bad feelings, or dubious actions, which can actually be understood as tugs for attention from the Boyfriend Within, as symptoms calling for a cure. It's uncomfortable to have a real-life boyfriend suddenly confronting you angrily at an unexpected moment. But if the confrontation leads to the solution of a conflict you've been ignoring, the momentary unpleasantness is worthwhile in the long run. Some of the sorts of feelings or behavior often indicating you're out of sync with, or, in other words, having problems with your Boyfriend Within are: compulsive behavior, such as lingering for hours in on-line chat rooms, or smoking

a half-pack of cigarettes; feeling exaggeratedly out-
raged at a guy spending too long filling his water bottle in front of you at the fountain at the gym; not
being able to concentrate at work, or in conversations.
The most common and deeply felt siren sounding
from within, though, probably remains those blues
about being lovelorn, or otherwise unhappy in romantic love.

I recently ran into a deejay friend of mine, Rick,
who pedaled up to the curb on his bicycle to tell me
he'd been listening to old tapes from The Saint, the
prime gay New York City disco of the early 1980s. "All
the songs are these masochistic love songs about
wanting love and not getting it and getting dirt kicked
in your face by your beloved," he complained, almost
in a rant, his industrial tattoos peeping from under a
gray muscle shirt. "It was four or five in the morning.
These guys were really vulnerable. They were in a
dance trance under the influence of drugs. And they
were being brainwashed and being told over and over
that love is all about suffering and crying and losing. I
think that's why all these gay men go around behaving like immature high school girls!"

I'm not so sure about the "immature high school
girls" part, but Rick was definitely onto something.
Not that gays have a total monopoly on the attitude

he was describing. The masochistic love song has always been a staple of the music industry. For Diana Ross, love was a hangover for which she didn't want a cure. Prince tabulated the precise count of a lover's departure down to an agonizing "seven hours and fifteen days" in "Nothing Compares 2 U." More than once, Sarah Vaughan made famous songs that were variations on the theme of "The One I Love Belongs to Somebody Else."

I wouldn't want to naïvely point away from the three-way intersection where the often beautiful, sometimes bloody collision can occur between pain, suffering, and beauty. Too much creativity can be traced to that particular accident site. For instance: on the occasion of conducting Handel's *Messiah* for the one-hundred-sixty-ninth time at Carnegie Hall during the Christmas season, David Randolph confessed to *The New York Times* that his relationship with the oratorio had begun at age seventeen, when he was informed by Walta, a girl he loved, that she felt only friendship for him. To ease the embarrassment of the moment, they stepped into a church on lower Fifth Avenue, where a musical performance was in progress. The first sound they heard was a sad melody, a tenor singing the words, "Thy rebuke hath broken his heart." "This was my first exposure to Handel's *Messiah*," he told the *Times*. "I would love to know what has happened to Walta in the intervening six decades and to tell her I perforce thought of her one-hundred-sixty-eight times."

As Randolph's story shows, life has a way of coming up with its own suffering, challenges, disappointments, and rejections. And people occasionally have a way of turning them around. But that doesn't mean there's an imperative to manufacture an extra supply of dross in hopes of accruing an extra supply of gold. The Pollyannaish claim that everything will work out fine if properly approached, or positively thought about, is obviously off. But so is the popular idea that great art can *only* come from suffering or being driven to an early death. The recipe for great love doesn't always have to include obsession, compulsion, and the discomforting feeling of being poised on a cushion of pins and needles.

In this chapter I won't be dealing so much with those essentially tragic situations that are part of the existential infrastructure—war, incurable disease, death: These may or may not be beyond the ken of human wish and choice. Rather, I'll be treating those matters of concern that are still within the purview of our own choice and accountability, things which intimately concern the Boyfriend Within insofar as he's involved with matters of the heart. For it's the heart that sounds the alarm when the Boyfriend Within is troubled. And it's the heart that registers happiness when that positive state occurs. If the Boyfriend Within lives anywhere, he lives in the heart.

Awareness Exercise Eight

List at least five uncomfortable feelings that have made your heart hurt, or made you dizzy enough with fear and anxiety that you couldn't think straight, or have caused you to feel apprehension in your gut. Next to this list of feelings, write down short notes to remind you of actual, remembered situations to which you can connect them. We don't, after all, just have feelings, we have situational feelings.

When checking my own list of crazy patterns in earlier Awareness Exercises against my friends and informants lists, I was always entertained by their variety and dissimilarity. In the lists of troubling emotions, however, I found my own to be almost universally the same as everyone else's. Modulations occur more generally in the spelling out of the situations that create these feelings in different people.

My short list of downers and the situations that helped kick them in included:

- **Hurt**—not invited to a party; overlooked for a promotion at work
- **Angry**—kept waiting an extra fifteen minutes by a workout partner; stood up when someone with whom I had a movie date decided to go dancing instead without bothering to call
- **Jealous**—being the odd man out in a conversation; hearing secondhand about my boyfriend on vacation with an Israeli soldier at the Dead Sea when I thought he was working on a movie in Geneva
- **Lonely**—just walking down the street

The first reaction to doing this exercise is often a heartfelt "Ugh." Some of my casual respondents hadn't been completely comfortable describing their "package" in the earlier Awareness Exercise in chapter 2, but those discomforts were funny, involving a sort of hesitation that seemed humorous. Wading into less pleasant emotions is a bit tougher. But again, it's ground that needs to be cleared. It's a room, as it were, that needs cleaning. Once you have your list and have written down accompanying memories, you'll be able to pick yourself up again. Not that there won't be rough moments in life ever again. But you'll see that a more buoyant and productive condition will be more consistently possible.

In the next exercise we'll be reshooting the primal scenes that we've allowed to bother us and to send us into these downward spins. And by reshooting them, we'll be able to change, thankfully, their emotional tenor and, thus, to expand our emotional options for the future. A wise, tough art history professor once told me—vis-à-vis I forget what—"You choose your feelings." Her comment made no sense to the eighteen-year-old me. By working on the next exercise, however, I began to experience directly what she meant and to put her meaning into action.

Awareness Exercise Nine

Revisit the territory of each of the feelings listed above and each of the situations from which they sprang, then reimagine them. That is, instead of the usual tack of simply reliving, returning again and again to the scene of the crime searching for the culprit responsible for such unfairness, just re-create things differently. It doesn't matter whether you write down your thoughts in full sentences or in short phrases that mean something mostly to you. The point is to try to think how you could have handled those moments differently to create a different emotional result. Use your notes as cues to re-visualize, or as I've said, borrowing a metaphor from the movies, reshoot the scene.

Here are a few of my notes on different situations. You're free, though, in this exercise to have pages and pages of thoughts:

- **Hurt**—not invited to a party

    Reshooting: Maybe the invitation went to the wrong address. Send change-of-address cards.

    or,

    Reshooting: Reviewing the list from the point of view of the hostess, I find that all the guests can help her get ahead in life in ways I can't. She's not thinking *against* me; she's just not thinking of me at all.

- **Angry**—stood up for movie date by someone who didn't call, didn't even apologize

    Reshooting: Expunge him from the credits; recast his part as moviegoing companion with someone more reliable.

- **Jealous**—being the third man out in a conversation

    Reshooting: Imagine what I *might* have said to

interject myself back into the conversation, such as, "Istanbul is my favorite city." Or, "There's going to be more income generated by video games than by movies within five years." Spin words off the top of my head. Next time, talk loosely this way rather than worrying.

- **Lonely**—walking down the street
  Reshooting: Take out my cell phone and line up a date, even if out walking with my BFW when the sensation hits. Make dates until sated and all I want is to be back in Garbo-land.

Experiencing gnawing emotions is certainly not a sign of lack of privilege, standing, or success. It's not the provenance of losers and geeks. In a "Talk of the Town" item in *The New Yorker,* for instance, a well-known art dealer revealed for an entire group of achievers the dynamics of hurt, jealousy, and general paranoia at work in a week of glamorous opening parties for the Getty Museum in L.A. His comments raised the possibility that insecurity actually can be exacerbated by approval and public success. "I have some friends who want to know every person on the guest list so that they can torment themselves as to whether or not they are at the right thing," he said. "I am told it is Richard Meier's night." (The art dealer was himself a guest on that "right" Tuesday night, the night devoted to guests of Meier, the museum's architect.)

I've shared a few of my easier and more straightforward examples. Now, if you're faced with the situation—as I was—of a lover of several years on a secret date in the Middle East, then you might need to think more deeply. Although the lover might be cast as the villain in the scene when it is considered in isolation, the entire movie begins to require a lot of editing to make matters go right. That is, his little fillip of betrayal might actually be traced back to a compressed fist of distance, or resentment, or of lying stretching back into many earlier scenes over many earlier months or years. Extensive reshooting is a tall order, but not an impossibility. Next time, with what you know now, the plot might arc more smoothly in the auteur production of your own life.

I CAST this chapter about these bluesy emotions as "problems with my Boyfriend Within" because such troubling emotions are often signs of being out of touch with the source of happiness and love within. These negative feelings seem to be related to people and events. But they're often actually about an inner relationship that's gotten offtrack. Something's not aligned, and it's usually the mind and the heart. The Voice's prescription is really an indication of the need to become realigned: "You have to meet the Boyfriend Within where he lives, on his own turf." The problems are never with the Boyfriend Within per se. They're always with your relationship to him/her/x/y/z.

These warning signs can also be detected in actions. We all have ways of acting out that help us avoid the tough work of feeling negative emotions and trying to turn them around. E-mailing me on this topic of avoiding negative emotions through obsessive-compulsive behavior, one friend confided, "My first reaction is that for most guys out there the first thing we encounter are obsessive behaviors which preoccupy and keep us away from feeling emotions at all. Some good warning signs I've encountered over the years in that category would be obsessive partying; disco every weekend; obsessing about problems with lovers; obsessive cruising in bars, baths, anywhere the inexhaustible prospect of connection exists; habitual substance use; duh, obsessive buying; obsessive—oh I don't know—list making. . . . I guess the list goes on."

If you've been reading and working your way through this book, you've learned some reliable measures for dealing with emotional or mental crises. Some may have been presented as techniques already;

some, implied. Others may be your own home remedies, concocted during a lifetime of trying to keep your head above water, or in the process of reading about and getting to know better the source of rejuvenation and general therapeutic uplift you carry around like a spiritual battery pack within.

Awareness Exercise Ten

Write down the ways you've found to be most effective and most trustworthy for reestablishing your relationship with the Boyfriend Within during difficult times. That is, when your psychic alarm goes off, when calls for attention from the Inner B are manifested as dark clouds of gloom or panic or loneliness or low self-esteem, what best can you do? The four sorts of activities I've found to be the most helpful in reestablishing my relationship with the Boyfriend Within, in giving him the attention he needs to sail on, are:

- Active, creative expression
- Passive inspiration
- Conversations with the Voice
- Meditation

One sort of active, creative expression that works for me is writing poems. Coinciding often with the first crush of romantic love and the tingling, preliminary apprehension of death in adolescence, poetry can be a way of letting the drops of blood splatter where they may. For adults who don't go on to become masters of the craft, this art sometimes diminishes over time as the weapon of choice for bloodletting. But I still hold onto poetry as a choice response for a system in chaos, unable to focus, just needing to get "it" out. (Poetry, of course, has plenty of other more high-minded uses in the culture, including crossing beyond the set borders of language and thought.) Less formally freighted and often equally effective is just taking pen to paper and writing down on a pad, or in a journal, the swirl of distraught words until a calm clarity returns.

Creative expression doesn't need to be confined to writing. Other choices can be visual, visceral, or musical. You could try finger painting, for example. There's something about the sheer childishness of this activity that makes me feel I'm totally involved in getting at angst rather than trying to impress someone or make something that will be suitable for framing. (It's important to find ways to sidestep any feelings of performance or audience. You should be doing this for yourself.) Making collages—especially those incorporating photographs from childhood—can give shape and jagged significance to an unconscious jumble. Composing aleatory music on piano or drums or guitar helps. Even banging a tennis racket on a bed, or thumping a pillow, can be percussive, tribal, purgative. The important point is just to keep at it—painting or writing or thumping—until the mood has lifted.

A second useful activity for getting back in touch with the Boyfriend Within is that of more passive inspiration, by which I mean going for a little more of what the poet Keats called "wise passivity." That is, kick back and soak in whatever you've found to be helpful, consoling, or inspiring to you. Reading is certainly an example, although not just reading for reading's sake, or not even reading for pure entertainment's sake—as *relaxing* as a spin with Ann Rice's vampires or John Grisham's lawyers might be. I'm thinking more of those few books on the shelf that reliably have acted as a match to the sentimental pilot light of your heart. A few of my old faithfuls are: Rainer Maria Rilke's *Letters to a Young Poet;* Thomas Merton's *Seeds of Contemplation;* or, occasionally, even Marianne Williamson's *A Return to Love.*

Music is also famously a hot bath, a "charm / To make bad good," as Shakespeare wrote. Again, the music you choose might not be what you'd put on when a guest comes over. It might not even be what you critically consider to be the best music. Certainly the books I listed above aren't on my list of the great works of literature—but then *The Brothers Karamazov* is not a book I'd reach for in a crisis. I admire Richard Strauss's difficult musical composition *Metamorphosen* as much as the next "dead white European male," but in a crunch I tend more toward the religious or melodic: *Chant,* by the Benedictine monks of Santo Domingo de Silos, or Samuel Barber's mournful *Adagio for Strings.* Don't be afraid to short-circuit your critical capacities in an emergency. It's one of those lifesaving secrets that can be kept squarely between you and your best interests. You won't be graded on it.

I've certainly discussed the Voice quite a bit in these pages. Yet I feel that the Voice can never be overestimated. The ultimate payback is the day when you find yourself free enough of angst and distraction to take time to ask the Voice some of the big questions, such as those heading each chapter in this book. These are highlighted moments when you really begin to think for yourself. In this developing—in private— of opinions on ultimate values and direction, you're actually developing a philosophical home base, a world of experience and meaning to share with your

Boyfriend Within. It might sound crazy, but it's truly (I think) as sane as it gets.

Meditation, too, can soothe a savage breast. What I now think of as meditation has developed in my own life from childhood prayers and from time spent in a contemplative Trappist monastery, and extends through to Eastern meditative techniques learned from books, seminars, and yoga classes. The sort of meditation you need for getting in touch with the BFW has little to do with magical acts of transcendence. You don't need to stand on your head atop a cold mountain. Certainly for advanced practice you would want to become part of a group, or hook up with a teacher with whom you feel comfortable, but for getting back in touch with the Boyfriend Within, the basics work fine.

Meditation as I'm envisioning the activity for the purpose at hand is just sitting quietly with the Boyfriend Within. It's spending time together. I try to do this for a half hour each day. First I read a bit. I run through a sort of checklist of conscience, of wishes and goals. It's my warm-up. This is also a good time for a back-and-forth with the Voice. Then I settle into simply breathing, following the rhythm of inhalation and exhalation, trying to let go of all the thoughts of the day. If distractions come up, and I find that I'm off and running after them, I breathe more deeply, erase the chalkboard as it were, and patiently begin over again. Breathing in. Breathing out. Often an involuntary smile will come over my face. That's a sign of progress—a sort of "hello" from the Boyfriend Within. Rather than finding the solution to a particular problem, the idea is that you have a feeling of relationship with your own source of power and contentment within, which is a general solution to almost all of the problems presenting themselves each day.

Some people establish a routine of meditating at a certain time every day, in a certain room, on a certain pillow. The repetition helps them return more easily, by power of suggestion and habit, to the state of mind associated with that time and place. I tend to meditate in the same room, on the same pillow, but at different times, according to convenience. Certainly if I'm feeling out of alignment with my Boyfriend Within, I use meditation as an emergency measure to get back in touch, whenever and wherever I am. If practiced regularly, meditation can become an agreed-upon meeting place between you and your Boyfriend Within. Of course, so can all of the practices I've listed, as well as other practices you may have invented and listed for yourself. For one friend, swimming is always the answer. Trust the ones that work for you.

•   •   •

My favorite contribution from street slang in the past year or so has been the phrase "Peace out!"—a perfect cap for describing the aftereffects of meditation in a world of action. It's an amalgam of the old hippie wish, "peace," with the "over/out" of, say, a jet fighter pilot. This mixed message allows the feeling of an open-ended blessing to come through benevolently, while maintaining some of the hard edge appropriate for a world in which war and peace, technology and spirituality must coexist.

If nothing else, the Rx of this chapter has called for peace-ing out, for withdrawing from an unequal struggle with self-created pain. By turning within, you'll be able to show up more naturally and effectively the next time you need to—for a person, or an event. *Out* is the natural direction for an overflow of peace that can come after time spent with the BFW, working through bad feelings or insecurity.

To quote the last line of a poem by the artist and poet Joe Brainard:

"PEOPLE OF THE WORLD: RELAX!"

Awareness Exercises:

8. List five uncomfortable, negative emotions. Next to the list, write down short notes about actual, remembered situations to which you can connect them.

9. Review the list of situations in Awareness Exercise Eight and write down notes for reshooting them to change their outcome.

10. List techniques for reestablishing your relationship with the Boyfriend Within that you've found to be most reliable in difficult times.

CHAPTER FIVE

QUESTION: *How does the Boyfriend Within relate to a Boyfriend Without?*

THE VOICE: *The Boyfriend Within will enhance your connection with your Boyfriend Without, not to mention with your Boyfriend(s) Without, your friendships and your partnerships.*

About two days after the Voice gave his answer to my question for this chapter, a photographer friend coincidentally announced to me on the phone: "This next year's going to be all about friendships and partnerships. That's where the lasting commitments come from. Those other kinds of relationships don't last. The needy, fake ones. The ones based on sex." I'm not denying there was a bitter tinge to his pronouncement, but there's no denying its essential wisdom either.

While mulling over this topic of the relevance of the Boyfriend Within to all the rest of our relationships, especially primary ones, I was serendipitously given a few more insights in conversations during the following weeks. It seemed appropriate that help in thinking about this subject come from voices outside—much like the photographer's sudden and unsolicited comment.

A second insight came from a psychotherapist who told me she'd conducted a group therapy session in New Jersey. A woman shared with the circle that after being divorced, she needed to find a new husband to help complete her new life. She went into cognitive therapy, attended singles' events, and ordered a sizable pile of books and videotapes on dating, courtship, and second marriages. One day, though, she woke up realizing that this second phase of her adult life was just fine without a new husband. Since that revelation she's actually remarried, but in the interim between the time of her realization and the event of actually meeting the right mate, she'd been content, relaxed, even flourishing. The change had certainly made her life easier. Perhaps by giving up on the aggressive, binocular-focusing search mode she had adopted, she paradoxically made the meeting of her second husband possible.

A third contribution came from a friend at a Sunday brunch. We began talking almost like anthropologists about the mating practices of gay men. Pretty soon the words and observations were tumbling so quickly, and overlapping so chaotically, that it's impossible for me to remember who said what when.

"What if we stopped going to bars and clubs and started looking to our friends for partners instead?"

"That happens sometimes. Guys have been friends for five years and then all of a sudden turn to one another and realize they've fallen in love without even trying."

"Is that crazy?"

"It's the reverse of the usual. Among gay men, sex is like a handshake, a way of saying hello. Then the sex often disappears gradually."

"Not always."

"Right, right. . . . But this way it would sort of grow from a glimmer to a gleam over months or years. It's a wild thought."

"Commitment might be more lasting that way. At least you'd know what you were getting."

"Less like Lotto?"

The gist here was that gay men often search outside their circle of friends for some equivalent of a tall, dark stranger. It's almost like a hunter going into the woods in search of his prey. Rather than kill it, however, the gay man drags back his exotic find, with whom he's become romantically involved. Often this tall, dark stranger eventually becomes domesticated and fits within the known circle of friends, thus changing his status from prey to fellow hunter, and the cycle begins again. (Of course such maneuvers occur in straight society as well, though more often marriage partners seem to be drawn from among friends of friends, or fellow guests met at a dinner party. Perhaps the particularly feisty man-man combination of gay male life—as opposed to man-woman—is responsible: Lesbians also seem to operate more often *within* an established social circle.)

Those three conversations all helped me to begin to clear up for myself the Voice's initially enigmatic-sounding answer to this question of what the Boyfriend Within could possibly mean to someone who's dating, or involved in a relationship: "The Boyfriend Within will enhance your connection with your Boyfriend Without, not to mention with your Boyfriend (s) Without, your friendships and your partnerships."

The basic concept behind the Boyfriend Within is simple, universal, and commonsensical—happiness comes largely from within. Certainly this is true to a greater extent than our culture generally appears to accept. Because of the commonsense aspect of this belief, we perhaps have a tendency to take its implications too lightly, to think it simply can be assimilated and then worn casually. But actually there is a domino effect that comes into play here, and it can have a substantial impact. Once we begin changing our attitude toward ourselves, we necessarily begin changing our attitudes toward others and toward the meaning of our friendships and love affairs and long-standing commitments. That is, if you go there, you'll begin in the ensuing months to reevaluate much more than your personal moods and habits—the effects can be far reaching and complex.

The Boyfriend Within turned out for me to be a sort of Archimedes' lever. The world that could be measured by the concept expanded gradually from a personal to an interpersonal one. The need for change had been signaled in the beginning in a negative way: I felt I couldn't connect; my circuitry was fouled up. Now the change was beginning to be signaled in a positive way. I began to feel . . . well . . . friendlier. The repercussions of that friendliness are the stuff of this chapter.

If you believe that your own happiness is dependent on someone else, you are going to give that person a lot of control over you—power to make you happy, power to frustrate you, and power to destroy you emotionally. A prospective mate can suddenly have license to behave in ways unacceptable for anyone else in your life. But if you keep the stress on the second syllable—emphasizing the "friend" in "boyfriend"—you can begin to lighten up and have your wits about you as well. This doesn't mean that romance won't ever strike. But you will come to appreciate a new acquaintance for exactly who he is, not for how close he comes to delivering word-for-word the script you've assigned him in the play of your life—a play which, if staged on that principle, would be a revival at best. Rose-colored glasses don't always make things look better after all, just more baroque.

By our starting off on a friendlier footing, the basis on which we carry on a relationship can then shift. It's like the adjustment described in the old wives' saying about marriage: "The first time is for love, the second time for money." What's meant by "love" in this context is probably fireworks at midnight, over Central Park on New Year's Eve, viewed from the perfectly located crystal bay window. That is, romance. But what's meant by "money" can perhaps be broadened to include a few things other than cash in the bank—job, achievement, access to a compatible social world. It might sound harsh and unvalentinelike of the Voice to appear to be bringing deal making and business into the discussion, but then love and friendship, if they're real, are grounded in body as well as soul, bank as well as bed, persona as well as person.

Addressing the question of relationships is at least as complex as addressing everyone's Inner B, because different readers are involved in different sorts of relationships, or are situated at different points on the life curve. Basically, though, there are three choices, each of which *I've* certainly opted for in some form at one time or another: married; single; dating. The relationship of the Boyfriend Within to the first two is relatively straightforward. As dating is a more fluid experience, the relationship between the inner and the outer boyfriend in this third case becomes more fluid, complex, and strategic. If you're involved in one situation, you're certainly free to skip the Awareness Exercises targeted for a different situation. But then curiosity about what your peers are up to might draw you in. For most of us, all three cards tend to be played eventually.

"Married"

"Marriage" for gay people is still an open-ended institution. It remains, as Melville said of life, "a voyage out," rather than a trip with a defined itinerary. Statistics indicate that in our society, the institution of marriage continues, but under the sign of the question mark. High divorce rates indicate ambivalence and confusion. Yet, just when straight couples are chafing under the restraints of marriage agreements, many gay political leaders are struggling to make the institution available to all. Jurisprudence in Hawaii appears ready to allow gay marriages. The State of New Jersey is now permitting two men to jointly adopt a child—a sideways form of tentative, indirect approval.

Across the nation, a few gay men have been married in a civil, lay, or religious ceremony; more have exchanged "friendship rings." For most, however, "marriage" is self-defined: You're married if you say you're married. For purposes of this book, when I'm discussing marriage, I'm speaking of being in a primary relationship with one person in which there's some mutual understanding of commitment coupled with a long-term view, even if there's an awareness of the flexibility and fragility of such vows and views;

that is, of the quixotic nature of the noble enterprise. Certainly my eleven-year relationship, including seven years of living together, was in many ways like a marriage.

I went to a traditional wedding ceremony once where the officiating priest, in his short homily to the bride and groom, interpreted the line, "I take this man to be my lawful wedded husband. . . ." He said that what it largely meant was that "I *don't* take Jack, or Fred, or Barney. . . ." That is, the commitment to one person is implicitly a giving up of lots of other people, at least as a wife or husband. (Episcopalians have never been much for harems or polygamy.) One of the signs of being in a more "married" state is that others have been excluded from that particular niche of heart and life. The deal in terms of how involved you may become with those others—Jack, or Fred, or Barney—is then worked out case-by-case by each couple, either together or unilaterally, in negotiation or on the sly.

"Letting go" forms a significant undertow to being married, or even to just the feeling of being married. "It's like letting go of the handlebars," someone once remarked to me of the trust and commitment involved. By stepping onto the same vessel and floating away from shore, a couple's opportunity for a mutually focused adventure is made more possible. Somehow the wind in the sails is this very commitment to one course and the abandonment of shorter, more varied day trips. Yet once underway and "out at sea" so to speak, rough moments arise. Even in the closest of marriages, solitude and aloneness recur. It's at these moments that the Boyfriend Within can make his helpful presence known, becoming a stand-in, surrogate, companion, or guide.

Awareness Exercise Eleven

List a few occasions in your life with a Significant Other when you suddenly felt thrown back on your own resources, or left alone. Then using the skills you used in the Awareness Exercises in the last chapter, make notes for reshooting the scene: Write down how you might have handled the situation differently—or even just thought about the situation differently—if you'd been as tuned in to the Boyfriend Within as you're hopefully becoming by now. (Remember that such reshooting isn't just wishful thinking, fantasy, or imagination. It may directly change the way these scenes will play themselves out in the future at unexpected junctures.)

I found that my list, and those of a few of my

friends, usually contained three types of potential wake-up calls. The first tend to be work-related separations, and these are the easiest for the Boyfriend Within to help salvage:

- I was "married" to a filmmaker who was forever going away on shoots that could last for weeks, or even months, here and abroad.
- I was later involved with an actor who would enter into speeded-up, intense periods of work.
- A friend's boyfriend, an architect, recently went to work in Toronto for three months.
- Another's boyfriend of several decades has moved to the Carolinas simply because he could not function anymore in the city: They spend a weekend a month, and large chunks of vacation time together.

The reshooting of these moments usually involves some version of the dating of the Boyfriend Within concept from chapter 3. The reaction of the partner "left behind" in these situations can be that he's left holding the bag, or keeping the home fires burning. Such curatorial work is ego challenging. Suddenly you feel you're a minor employee rather than a full partner in the firm. Many of the kinder, gentler customs of being together—simply keeping the place tidy, making sit-down meals, taking a movie break—are found to have been based on being a couple. A more positive revision of these feelings can come about by using this time for intensive sessions with the Boyfriend Within (checking in with the Voice every hour?) and for learning to make life comfortable and cushioned not just for an *us,* but for you (videos for one?).

In one of my own examples for Exercise Eleven, for instance, my solution for reshooting was clearly evident to me in retrospect:

- My filmmaker boyfriend was away for five
  months, working in Europe.
    Reshooting: Instead of cursing him under my
  breath, or feeling mopey and lonely, I use the
  opportunity to redecorate; to take lessons in
  northern Italian cooking and put them to good
  use; to have a party.

More challenging are those situations of the second type, in which you feel you're being insensitively upstaged, or you're dealing with problems of your partner's that only become yours by proxy. I've been disturbed when:

- A lover came home hours late
- He didn't come home at all
- He went off for an extended weekend in the country with someone else

First off, these more serious ruptures require talking things out with your partner, and perhaps even counseling. You have to know what you've agreed to in the first place. If vows are being flippantly broken, then it's definitely time to talk. If differences are irreconcilable, you can always choose to move on. For example:

- He didn't come home at all.
  Reshooting: Instead of turning my face to the wall for a few days, we talk when it first happens; if there's a second time, we check into couples' counseling.

Either way, you can use these upsets as additional opportunities to take care of yourself. Often the feeling that "He doesn't love me"—whether justified by events or not—is a warning-in-disguise from within that you're not loving *yourself* enough. Much anger and frustration can be dissipated by simply dropping everything for a good, long session of loving self-indulgence. After this soul sifting, take care of whatever problems remain.

The third sort of problems are profound dilemmas that can take away the body, or spirit, of a partner. Examples are:

- AIDS
- Drug dependency
- Depression

These more extraordinary situations require the taking on of an additional role with your partner so you're able to be an effective nurse, tough-love coach, or angel. The Boyfriend Within now becomes more of a special energy source that can be tapped for its supply of heat, energy, love, and compassion. The more serious the problem, the more profound and mystical the qualities required of, and usually provided by, the BFW. Cultivate him now if you want to be assured of being delivered during such crises later.

- Drug dependency
  Reshooting: Instead of thankfully watching him shuffle off to scream therapy, I become involved in his therapy and start a focused program of my own to examine why I allowed

myself to pretend I didn't know about the problem, or felt unable to help him overcome it.

Finally, in marriage you must respect your partner's Boyfriend Within as scrupulously as you do your own. Otherwise there'll be trouble. I had a partner who decided to fly by himself to a resort of chic shacks on the beach in Jamaica for New Year's. I couldn't believe he didn't want to take me. Was he really going to read those four bestselling novels he packed? My mind played tricks about who he was meeting, and why. I found it much harder to sincerely believe that *his* Boyfriend Within was asking for time and space— with no particular reflection on me—than to listen to the sometimes irrational wishes of *my* BFW. It turned out that he really was simply off on his own no-pressure holiday.

Single

In a sense this entire book has been a meditation on the nature of being single, since we're all somewhat single even if married or dating. It's been an updating and hopefully a deepening of one of the first successful self-help books, Helen Gurley Brown's *Sex and the Single Girl,* from the sixties. Of course "Sex" by now has evolved to "Sex, Romance, Love, and Spirituality," and "The Single Girl" to "The Singular Guy/Girl." And just my comfort at being able to telegraph to you such a boggling notion at this point means that this section can be short, a tying up of a few loose ends. That is, you already know it all.

Awareness Exercise Twelve

Write a paragraph in which you express why you've chosen to be—or by accident or design have found yourself—single at this moment in your life. If you're not single, write a paragraph in which you express why you've chosen not to be.

Here are my thoughts on the subject:

- By looking within rather than without for happiness, love, and support, I've coincidentally drained a lot of the air out of my tires as far as the old motivations go for looking for a boyfriend, lover, partner, mate. I now enjoy all my partnerships and friendships in all their subtle colorings and shadings. If one of these relationships should grow into something more primary, or more romantic, I'd obviously be happy and pleasantly surprised. More power to us. But I'm not beginning with the end in mind.

Your thoughts on being single, your point of view on this existential condition, will be especially crucial in determining the quality of your life should you decide to move on to the next phase, dating.

Dating

To date well, to discover the Zen of dating, you need to be flexible. You need to be having fun. I didn't always feel that way before I meditated and acted on the notion of the Boyfriend Within—until its repercussions became part of my own experience. In fact I often said "I don't date." And I often didn't. Partly the notion seemed corny and better left to teenagers—a time in my life when my dates with girls were disasters of shyness, subterfuge, embarrassment, and ineptitude. But mostly, in my adult life, I'd decided that dates were the equivalent of job interviews. That both partners were really interviewing each other for a certain job with a certain job description. The slacker in me just couldn't participate. I balked.

AWARENESS EXERCISE THIRTEEN

Whether married, single, or dating, make a short list of four or five people you'd *like* to date. They can be famous. They can be crushes. They can be sexual or nonsexual attractions. They can be people already in your life who you simply enjoy being with for no particular reason. Indeed, "for no particular reason" is important here. This one exercise is simply about having fun, taking a break. Just because you're already going out with someone doesn't mean you want him on this list. You should make this a completely irresponsible wish list, not a test to see how you view yourself, and certainly not a list of people with whom you'd necessarily want to make a life commitment. It's a list that probably would be completely different five days from now, five months from now, even five minutes from now. For comic relief, you can even add a movie star. Consider it more as a mood ring than a wedding band. At best, it will help take the edge off an activity that has perhaps become *overly* weighted with import.

My list, off the top of my head, a Polaroid of a moment of wishful mental time, is:

- Brian
- Keanu Reeves
- Bret
- Tough Thug (on-line screen name)

Feel free to mix gay and straight, men and women, people you really know and movie stars. Or not.Be as conservative or as radical as you want at the moment.

THE revelation in my own life has been the discovery that the source of security and pleasure many of us have been searching for is probably at the center of our lives rather than spinning on the periphery. This revelation had its most palpable aftershocks in my dating life, and more profoundly in my entire view of relationships with guys, girls, friends, boyfriends, lovers, and even business partners. I'm sure the Boyfriend Within is universal, no matter what name he goes under. I'm not so sure that the implications I've found concerning the Boyfriend Without will *necessarily* be your implications. That's between you and your Voice. But I suspect they might be.

What happens when you stop expecting to find

the qualities of your Boyfriend Within in a Boyfriend Without? And what are the implications for dating? And for your life? A first response might be, to reiterate the words of a bluesy number, "Is that all there is?" Or the ambiguously slanted title of a recent movie about romantic oscillation, *As Good As It Gets*—meaning that when you finally land on your feet, there's a sinking feeling of nowhere left to go. You're a disappointed Alexander the Great with no more lands to conquer. Hunting season has been declared over. So what to do now on weekends?

Awareness Exercise Fourteen

List real or possible reactions to the condition of no longer looking at the world as a mail-order catalog from which you're hoping to pick out the best possible boyfriend. If you stop shopping, you might feel let down at first. But other interesting feelings might soon begin to well up to fill the void. For some, including me, the world begins to open out more and more into that sixties paradigm: "a better place."

Among the discoveries I've made, and you might make:

- Suddenly looking romantically at a friend of ten years
- Hanging out almost exclusively with people who make me feel good, who excite me, or who seem emotionally open and available; not doing the reverse—hanging onto a chore of a person for the sake of a "relationship"
- Sleeping with friends; or conversely, spending more time with someone to whom I'm romantically attracted, but, for one reason or another, I won't be sleeping with anytime soon, if ever

I'm emphasizing the "fun" involved here because many interested parties have expressed fears about going too far with the Boyfriend Within. "It sounds like you're giving up sex and romance," someone complained. "Who wants that?" Actually, though, sex and romance remain very much present, perhaps even more pervasively present when you begin to dance with partners while keeping centered on the Boyfriend Within. Rather than being easily labeled, sex and romance become a more volatile, mysterious part of everyday encounters. In essence, you bring all the adrenaline and excitement of the hunt in the dark woods into the circle of your daily life. Everyone's circle can become charmed. It's a kind of white magic.

I'm not denying the difficulties here. Living against the grain takes some spunk and even more resilience. You're not always going to be up to the task. Sometimes you're going to forget about your BFW, or not be able to conjure him up, or even feel abandoned by him. That's when you might find yourself on some deserted street, stalking your fantasy at midnight during a full moon, and wonder how you got there. Or you'll be acting out your anxiety about a blank Friday night with nothing to do by playing too many video games, or smoking too many cigarettes, or drinking too many beers. If you begin to navigate by your Boyfriend Within, though, this too shall pass. You'll gradually come to be more and more under his influence, and your life will change by gradations. Just go easy on yourself during the inevitable periods of backsliding and regression. You'll soon be back on course.

The opposite concern is that this is all too easy, a mere concession to the Peter Pan complex of not wanting to grow up. It's true that allegiance to your Boyfriend Within can spare you many entangling adult responsibilities, but it will be only those that are self-defeating and slightly dishonest. Being freed in this manner is finally not a self-serving, rootless way to live. Indeed it's only when freed from needy, false love—from looking for love in all the wrong places— that a truly mature love can begin to grow.

Without the obvious calls to responsibility and other-directed behavior provided by a traditional wife or husband, children, or extended family, gay people sometimes appear to be living in a vacuum, in a self-referential spinning top of a "me" world. As I discuss in the next chapter, however, the Boyfriend Within eventually turns out—surprisingly, given the narcissistic-seeming tinge to the concept—to provide oxygen that can transform that very vacuum into commitment, contribution, and selfless service.

AWARENESS EXERCISES:

11. List a few occasions in your life with a Significant Other when you suddenly felt thrown back on your own resources, or left alone. Then write down notes about how you might reshoot the scene—how you might have handled, or even thought about, the situation differently.

12. Write a short paragraph in which you express why you've chosen to be—or by accident have found yourself at this moment—single. If you're not single, write a paragraph in which you express why you've chosen not to be.

13. Compose a wish list of at least four people with whom you'd like to go on a date.

14. List real or possible reactions to no longer looking at the world as a mail-order catalog from which you're trying to pick out the best possible boyfriend.

CHAPTER SIX

QUESTION: *What's love got to do with it?*

THE VOICE: *Love is the selfless work you do for another. Love makes you feel loved.*

ONE EVENING I was having supper at a macrobiotic restaurant with a playwright friend who was explaining to me more plaintively and stridently than usual why he particularly needed a boyfriend in order to lead a fulfilled life. I decided not to just nod sympathetically, but to get down in the trenches with him and try to work this through.

"What is it that you expect to get out of this relationship that's so different from what you get from your friendships?" I asked sincerely.

"I want to feel love," he said. "I want to love and be loved. It's not the same as friends."

"Well, if you want to have that feeling of love in your heart, why not volunteer to work in a soup kitchen or something?" I suggested.

My easygoing friend looked positively angry. His face burned reddish. One eyebrow peaked upward. I realized that I'd said the wrong thing, that I'd definitely pushed some button.

"I give back to the world through my writing," he shot back. "That's my contribution. I'm not talking about *that* kind of love."

I promptly dropped the subject. Now I probably would never have made such a lofty-sounding remark if I hadn't recently had an experience with the very phenomenon I was trying to discuss. What sounded like a non sequitur to my friend actually possessed a logic for me.

The inspiration I was drawing on for my unwelcome suggestion during our dinner of scrambled tofu and steamed vegetables had occurred during my then-recent New Year's retreat at the ashram in the Catskills. That's when I'd had my first experience with selfless service, or *seva* as it is called. During my five-day stay, our daily activities were supposed to include stopping by a central office to be assigned a few hours of unpaid duty for the community at large, such things as dishing out oatmeal in the cafeteria, serving as an usher in the main meditation hall. As a mark of service completed, you received a star pasted on your identification badge. This notion of *seva* rankled me at first, so much so that I resolved to steer clear. I wasn't going to be ripped off by having to perform mindless work for zero pay.

Curiosity, guilt, and boredom finally got to me, however. So on the last possible day I filled out a form with my qualifications. With no discernible reference to all those skills I'd snappily listed, I was assigned work on an upcoming musical pageant about a thir-teenth-century Hindu saint. My job was to tape pieces of black felt over chinks in the screens at the back of the stage. I learned how to cut swatches with a razor, thanks to an entertainment lawyer from L.A., and met a half dozen new people on the crew. That night at the production I couldn't help admiring the sheer black-ness of the backdrops and side drops. I felt strangely proud. And the community effort involved—the novelty of moving forward a project that wasn't my own—did leave a sweet, burning sensation in my heart.

I thought back to that uplifting session of cutting and taping while talking to the frustrated playwright, and to that time when I wrote down the Voice's answer to my question about love and the Boyfriend Within—"What's love got to do with it?" Click! I suddenly understood the leap involved in going from the question—which I'd been thinking of purely in terms of *romantic* love—to the answer. But it's a leap everyone can't necessarily follow at first.

"I need somebody to love," another friend said to me, echoing both the playwright *and* the Beatles. "I want somebody to love." If someone says this to you, and your first reaction is, "Well, go work in a soup kitchen," I can promise that you're not going to get very far. But the more you begin to think about the issue—with the help of a Boyfriend Within, strengthened by lots of attention over weeks and months—the more you might begin to arrive at an explanation, a justification that makes sense to you. But *only* if you've been regularly practicing love and care for the subtle needs of your Boyfriend Within all along. Just as you have to be twenty-nine before you're thirty, I don't think you can understand or create much love before you're thoroughly happy.

The oddity of my spiritual work-study program at the ashram had been the linking together of a feeling with a contradictory stimulus. The feeling was a glowing in the heart—which, of course, is the phenomenon of love. Such love is a one-size-fits-all response: It's the same whether evoked by a kiss, or the giving or receiving of a gift, or the adoption of a child, or a warm hug on a crowded street. It's the reward of caring. Boyfriends and lovers present each other lots of opportunities for creating this feeling: bringing home flowers, remembering a birthday, calling up and apologizing after a misunderstanding. But mundane life presents lots of opportunities too. Even dumb manual labor can be one of them, if the meaning is there.

If you're like the playwright, you've probably resisted the Voice's conclusion. Counting up cards received on Valentine's Day seems more appealing. Yet the more you think about it, the more convinced you may become that the Voice is onto something. Or more accurately, the more you *feel* your way into the subject, the more convinced you may become. This chapter is really about learning to be "warmhearted," which means learning to warm up your own heart and, by extension, those of others. To love and be

loved by the Boyfriend Within is to feel that warmth—
and to try to sustain its glow as long as possible.

Luckily you won't need to travel to an exotic, mul-
ticultural ashram in the Borscht Belt to activate this
love within—to set up a call-and-response dynamic of
love between you and your Boyfriend Within. You can
start where you live. And you don't even need to start
with a burning cause, or even a charitable organiza-
tion, church, mosque, or synagogue. The first circle
you can begin to heat up is the immediate one that
includes your friends, family, colleagues, and acquain-
tances. This is your circle of influence. It's been tailor-
made by you, for you. And those who loom largest
within its circumference are the perfect subjects with
whom you can begin to practice love.

"What's this?" I asked a freelance editor recently
as I sauntered over to his workstation in a corner of
his apartment. Stuck on the wall was a yellow Post-it
with the message, "Make one nonbusiness call today!" "Oh, that's just a reminder; if I don't see it, I
don't do it," he responded when I asked its significance. The reminder, he went on to explain, was designed to make him reserve one phone call a day—out
of the scores he makes as a freelance editor—to someone who was not a client, a business prospect, or a potential sex partner. He told me how rare such calls

had become in his life. And how satisfying the results of the calls when he made them. No matter how the recipient responded on the other end, he knew he was fueling his own fire. This was a kind of warmth he'd been missing before he began obeying his Post-it. Such "selfless" calling didn't come naturally at first. The force of resistance can be surprising. And yet the heart is structured as a matching fund. Give it an excuse, and you'll be feeling that initial warmth spontaneously several times afterward. That is, put one log on the fire, and you've got the equivalent of a Duraflame throughout the day.

What you're likely to find is that "selfless" action is really not selfless at all. It's self-ish, even, depending on your definition. I had a movie-actor friend who was in an car accident in L.A. He moved back to New York City for therapy and rehabilitation. Large chunks of his memory had been erased, at least temporarily. It seemed that getting together with him would be a chore. Some of his friends avoided him entirely. Taking my editor friend's Post-it suggestion, I put my actor friend's name on my list of charitable calls. Not only did I feel good for doing something without an immediate personal payoff, I discovered that our friendship—on the phone, in person—was as deeply rewarding as before in fun, communication, and even in fueling the slight crush I'd always had on him. I was getting double bang for my buck.

Well-meaning activity is in that special class of work that doesn't necessarily present its rewards up front. Physical exercise would be another. When my alarm clock goes off at 7:30 in the morning to rouse me to see my trainer, all I want to do is to press the snooze button. And yet by the time I've left the gym, I'm invariably energized. It's a gift I give to myself that keeps being rewarding throughout the day, and often over the next day or two. Yet if I followed my initial feeling about the enterprise, I wouldn't ever be there. Love and working out are similar in that way. You need to overcome an initial hesitation to get to the culminating goal.

The more love you make, the more love the Boyfriend Within will take, and give. Buckminster Fuller wrote somewhere that if you want to prevent highway accidents, you don't put up warning signs, you redesign the highway so that it's curved in such a way as to prevent accidents. In the following exercise we're thinking of ways in which you can build curves into your own personal highway to arrive at a more loving destination and to have a more loving and heartwarming trip getting there. While the notion of a warm heart might sound *merely* sentimental, it may well turn out in a study in a medical journal someday to exhibit positive biochemical results as well. But that's mostly just a guess on my part.

Awareness Exercise Fifteen

This exercise allows us to begin to design our own workout program for love. The first half is concerned with noticing how far you've come, perhaps without even keeping score. I don't know anyone who hasn't been practicing love in their lives to some extent. It seems to be an instinct. The second half of the exercise is concerned with devising new ways in which you can make room for even more love, and for its resulting advantages in your life.

To reflect the split agenda in this exercise, take a blank sheet of paper and draw a line down the middle. Label one side "Past" and the other side "Future." On the "Past" side, write down those times in your life when you've done extra work for love's sake. Your examples can be great or small, accidental or resolved, successful or overlooked. But I'm sure they're there. On my own list:

- Taking care of Howard when he was sick
- Helping a friend move

- Calling a sick acquaintance in the hospital
- Writing a thoughtful and explicit condolence card

Jumping out from the list in importance to me would be the first item: taking care of Howard when he was sick. Sickness and death are universal opportunities for care and service, of course. Certainly for gay men over the past decade, few calls have been more pressing than caring for those sick with AIDS. Especially during the earlier years of the medical crisis, the victims seemed cruelly fated to death camp–like horrors, some of which have been mitigated by developments in treatments since. I lived through one intense experience of caring. Many others—especially in New York City, Los Angeles, and San Francisco—have volunteered for a half dozen such cycles of rising and falling hopes and fears. And continue to do so.

Particularly relevant to this chapter is the payoff of such an experience and the realization of unexpected inner resources somehow made available for the task. I'm the type who, on principle, never would have volunteered for such service. Mother Teresa I'm not—and ten years ago, I was much less so. Almost every night before going to the hospital—during Howard's two lengthy hospital stays—I'd lie on my bed in my apartment having stomach cramps and a private tantrum before leaving. I just wanted to flee to a dirty movie theater, or to Palm Springs. And yet Howard maintained an astounding amount of wit and bravery. And our intimate capsule grew to be as fulfilling and satisfying as it could be stultifying, confining, and life stopping. The closer we came to death, the more on fire my heart seemed, and his, seemingly, as well. As a caregiver, I had direct experience of the paradox pointed to by the Voice: "Love makes you feel loved."

Now, on the second half of your page, labeled "Future," write down plans of action to experience this paradox of love if it isn't forced on you. For those who've been affected by the experience of being a caregiver, think how you can now seek out such opportunities so as not to lose what you gained. For those fortunate enough to have missed such a difficult lesson, think how you can begin to seek opportunities to exercise love in your own world. In these matters, remember, proportion is largely irrelevant. Small gestures can count as much as big. My own list of tactics on the "Future" side of my page includes:

- Follow my friend's example by making one nonbusiness call a day, a call based purely on love or friendship

- Give money on impulse to people or causes that move me—including tips to sympathetic waiters, cabdrivers
- Keep my ears tuned to people asking for favors, and consider saying yes rather than no automatically
- At least *reply* to unsolicited letters, gifts, invitations, rather than treating them as hostile interruptions

Most obvious to me in my "Future" list is its humbleness in scale compared to the "Past" list. But such humble goals can be rationalized. Love, or even simple kindness, is ambitious enough—the rewarding emotional honey coming after rather than before the experience. In place of the romantic model of fireworks, roses, and bells ringing, we have instead the less-seductive model of the frog that needs to be kissed to turn into a prince. That is, gratification is delayed. Works of love are matters of faith based on experience. So beginning small can be a good way to keep from being disappointed and put off early on. My own list of resolutions could be reduced to one simple theme: Bring down the wall!

•   •   •

GOING public follows naturally from private acts of love. It's the nature of love to want to find new expression. While I've been writing this, I've been watching out my window as two elderly gentlemen— one in a wheelchair—have been trying to flag down a taxi. Most of the yellow cabs simply whizzed past the problem situation. A few paused to consider the request before driving off. Finally one driver, who appeared to be of Caribbean origin, stopped to do the extra work of helping the two men into his cab, then loading the wheelchair into the trunk—before his meter could begin its ticking. A driver practiced in the ways of love would be much more likely to stop than one who wasn't yet in the groove. Like aerobics, or weight lifting, or dancing the night away, love is a learned habit.

The public expression of loving requires an even bigger step than the private expression. And the immediate emotional payback can be even more uncertain. In this case, trial and error is usually indicated. I was a member of an Episcopal parish in Manhattan for several years. One of my duties there was to feed the homeless—arriving early on Sunday morning to prepare tuna fish sandwiches, then standing on the steps of the church afterward to hand out the lunches to a line of obviously needy people. This was good and necessary work.

Personally, though, I've found the most visceral satisfaction in gay-related volunteerism. I think that the gay community has an advantage in being able to find opportunities for volunteering that are underexposed, personally stimulating, and implosive. If you're gay, and you travel to cities abroad, you have the chance to check into a local gay bar or café and meet locals in a way a straight tourist can't always manage as easily. Similarly in the sphere of volunteerism there are lots of activities, both intimate and communal, where you can see the benefits of whatever extra effort you make in ways often denied to those simply writing checks to support large causes such as finding a cure for cancer or muscular dystrophy—not that those causes can't offer heartwarming activities too, especially for those who've lost friends or family to one of these diseases.

Awareness Exercise Sixteen

List activities that are worthy and exciting *possibilities* for your own volunteerism, if and when you're ready. You may initially feel you don't have enough time. You may be pressured by an overload at work. But first just try to see how many possible activities you come up with. You might even invent a few not yet tried that you see a place for. The more personal your list, the more opportunity you'll have of finding an activity that's right for you. On my list:

- Join "The Next Generation," a mentoring program for gay and lesbian students at Columbia University
- Volunteer for one of the outreach programs at Hetrick-Martin Institute
- Give money to, or take part in, benefits for programs for AIDS research or care, such as CRIA (Community Research Initiative on AIDS) or God's Love We Deliver
- Start a monthly discussion group in my home on gay spirituality

I find it significant that two of the programs of interest to me are transgenerational. The chance to jump generations is special. Part of the kick of being a parent or teacher is being in touch with a new generation—learning the lingo, finding out what music or video game is popular, getting the satisfaction of sharing any bits of common sense or wisdom picked up over the years. For single people who aren't parents, haven't adopted, or don't have teaching jobs, this pleasure is harder to find. Programs that involve adults mentoring younger people provide a reliable dose of this kind of exchange. The emotional return can be immediate and up front. And of course the value for those to whom you're giving your time is obvious. It's an example of a kind of volunteerism that has special nurturing values for gays and lesbians.

The friend who turned me on to "The Next Generation" program, a spin-off of GHAP (the Gay Health Advocacy Project) at Columbia University, found its get-togethers of gay adults and college students as exciting for him as for the students. "It's great to have your experiences be of value to someone else," he explained. "And to let these kids know of the support network that's out there. Talking with them never felt patronizing to me. I was able to easily respect them. There was a mutual freshness to be offered." Certainly one of the surprises of hands-on volunteering, especially in service to others, is the constant discovery that the refreshment is so often, as my friend so naturally put it, "mutual."

The Hetrick-Martin Institute in New York City is custom-made for such hands-across-the-generations excitement and fulfillment. It's an appropriate spot for those whose nurturing urges are being cramped by a lifestyle of too much "me." This nonprofit social center and school serves lesbian, gay, bisexual, and transgender youth, including homeless youth, young people with HIV, and all youth coming to terms with their sexuality. Volunteers can't be counselors, but they help at the after-school Drop-In Center, or Project First Step, reaching out to teenagers on the streets of the city, half of whom are gay or lesbian, many surviving by exchanging sex for money. If your city or town doesn't have anything of the sort, you might want to consider starting your own outreach to gay teens.

I dropped a "spiritual" activity into my own list because, ironically, I feel convinced that gays and lesbians—so often trashed by Christian fundamentalist groups—form one of the natural communities with a talent for ministry, liturgy, and an updating and deepening of spiritual life in this country, both for themselves and others. There's certainly a long tradition of single priests, nuns, prophets, shamans, and church organists to be tapped. I think that gays have particular promise for cultivating a new orchid of spiritual life, a successful hybrid, as long as it's attached to a plant rooted without denial in the black, erotic soil they've tilled so generously over the past few decades. Certainly everyone's Boyfriend Within has much to teach about how to proceed in such sincere and invisible matters.

Few parties are more exuberant than the Morning
Party held yearly on Fire Island, each year's splash
more extravagant, costumed, populated, and "done"
than the last. I'm all for morning parties . . . as well as
afternoon parties, evening parties, midnight dips, and
so on. There can never be enough. But I did have a
thought while staring out into that tanned crowd so
full of energy, life, and blatant financial and creative
resources: "What would it be like to take all of the
time, planning, and fire that went into this one day
and focus it, as rays through a magnifying glass, onto
other kinds of activity?" There's definitely a tremen-
dous amount of energy in the gay community that
has yet to be used and exploited, certainly in "selfless"
service in activities that will hopefully continue on
past the immediate crisis of AIDS. My perception
wasn't a put-down of the summer holiday's joy—just a
quick vision of something else, of extra possibilities.

Of course the Boyfriend Within responds to all
heartfelt contributing, regardless of the sexual orien-
tataion and gender of the recipient(s). He's an equal-
opportunity lover. Gay issues might have a special
resonance for some, but not for all. If your heart is
somewhere else, then that's where you're probably
going to want to look to experiment. Again, churches,
synagogues, and mosques have the longest associa-

tion with such voluntary labor—*seva* is a Hindu word, but hardly an exclusively Hindu activity. There are plenty of programs to choose from in every denomination—gays now even have their own denomination, the Metropolitan Community Church, which has its headquarters in Los Angeles. Political activity counts too. If you feel expansive marching at the Washington Mall for a larger cause, go *there*. Some art lovers feel fulfilled by volunteering to give tours at museums; book lovers by helping at the library. Satisfying options are as varied as are Boyfriends Within.

The key concept of chapter 3, on dating the Boyfriend Within, was, "To get to know the Boyfriend Within, you have to get outside yourself." This paradox has only been further unfolded in this chapter, beginning again with paradoxes from the Voice: "Love is . . . work. Love makes you feel loved." Volunteering is a comprehensive gesture of this understanding. We get to know and develop our relationship with the Boyfriend Within by actions—not by thoughts, words, whims, or moods. We need to make time and space if we are really to pass through the life changes made possible by this felt connection. Volunteerism can simply be thought of as the most fulfilling of dates with the Boyfriend Within. It's the one date that's guaranteed to be purely and simply about love.

Awareness Exercises:

15 Draw a line down the middle of a blank
    sheet of paper. Label one side "Past" and the
    other "Future." On the "Past" side write
    down those times in your life when you've
    done extra work for love's sake. On the
    "Future" side write down future possibilities
    for such good deeds in your own social
    circle.

16. List activities in the larger world that are
    worthy and exciting possibilities for your
    own volunteerism.

CONCLUSION

No one has written more beautifully or intricately about the Boyfriend Within than the thirteenth-century Persian poet Rumi. For several years, he'd experienced an intense friendship with a wandering dervish, Shams of

Tabriz, with whom he spent days and months at a stretch, talking and sharing late-night sessions of music, song, and dance. One day, however, Shams simply disappeared. Rumi, devastated by the loss, traveled to Damascus to search for his dear friend. In Damascus, he had an insight that altered his life and transformed him into one of the world's great poets:

> *Why should I seek? I am the same as*
> *he. His essence speaks through me.*
> *I have been looking for myself!*

In an introduction to *The Essential Rumi,* his translator appropriately capitalized both the words "Friend" and "Friendship" whenever referring to the beloved Shams.

Mystical poetry might have the reputation of concerning itself with flights of imagination or heightened experience not available to the ordinary person—the man in the Gap flannel shirt, as it were. Certainly anything thirteenth-century, Persian, or Islamic could excusably be thought exotic enough to put back on the shelf, slightly out of reach. But in fact Rumi in his thousands of poems describes the very experience of finding a Boyfriend Within, and his experience is available to anyone. In some people's lives, such transformation comes about seemingly without even trying. Chalk it up as one of life's lessons. In most cases, however, personal change requires help and takes time.

Hopefully by now you've encountered your own Boyfriend Within. We're all traveling from different directions yet can choose to arrive, finally, at a similar place—the place described by Rumi as "of Friend and friend." I was moved by the loss of a lover to AIDS and by a personal bout of self-questioning. Others have arrived at the same spot earlier or later in their lives, or they have gotten there out of quite different predicaments. I had lunch recently with someone I went to college with who's been in an open yet profound and binding relationship with his lover for twenty-five years. On the side, he dallied with several lightweight romances. But he confessed he'd lost his energy and enthusiasm for such thin mirages. He and his lover have been trying to learn to live with themselves in order to live more successfully with each other. This friend and I had reached some similar conclusions about sex and romance: he, "married"; I, single.

My own initial casting about was motivated by longing. I was longing for a lost friend, our relationship made more idyllic by the passing of time. I was longing, too, to meet a new provider of security, comfort, and happiness—a replacement. Such longing is hardly unusual. I find longing, more than any other theme, permeates gay poetry and fiction. Certainly this longing has been the motor of much human romance, love, politics, and history. But the actions and beliefs arising out of the feeling are not necessarily fixed and determined.

At the risk of sounding like a poor man's twelve-step program, this path of self-transformation I've outlined does have its own logic. If you've worked through the chapters and Awareness Exercises in this book, many of the discoveries and insights are behind you. And yet they are also ahead. For as you continue to consult the Voice—which for me has become a daily habit—and as you return to relevant sections of this book, you're free to mix and match discussions and exercises according to your own needs. It's helpful, though, to try to keep the entire scaffolding in mind.

Chapter 1 on "Why don't I have a boyfriend?" is a meditation on some of the wishes, lies, and dreams that follow from initial longing. Here we get a chance to locate the feeling of longing where it lives—within us. And we begin to locate its antidote of happiness and satisfaction within as well. The chapter is centered on demystifying the power of "boyfriend" as crutch, illusion, or confining role in our lives. Whether we're single or involved, this insight can free us up to begin to look within ourselves and outward to the world in a fresh way.

Chapter 2—"Who *is* the Boyfriend Within?"— brings the personal responsibility for finding our own Boyfriend Within into this work of self-discovery. Such work must necessarily be interactive because everyone's Boyfriend Within is slightly different, as is the unique combination of everyone's body type, blood type, perhaps astrological sign, and certainly genetic code. Some need peace and nurturing from their BFW. Others need permission to be wild and creative. Still others need adrenaline, a shot in the arm. This getting-to-know-you phase is active and introspective.

Chapter 3 on "How do I get to know the Boyfriend Within?" introduces the notion of dating. The real movement begins here, the back and forth, or "call and response." It's as if you've become a dance partner with yourself. The Boyfriend Within becomes not simply a notion, a catchy phrase, or even a feeling or a resolution. Time spent with the Boyfriend Within includes all the ups and downs, tugs and pulls of a dating cycle with a new friend. You need to make time and space. You need to commit.

Chapter 4 deals with the flip side: "What if I'm

having problems with my Boyfriend Within?" The Boyfriend Within is a blessing and an enhancement, but not a painkiller. He's unfortunately not psychic Prozac. And the choice to be sensitive to messages from within, like all human choices, must be considered as fitful and subject to change. We're still going to get the blues. There are times when we'd rather just shut down and suffer. Remember: We're adjusting our orientation here, not trading in our genus and species.

These interior adjustments wouldn't matter much if they didn't create changes in the way we live. Chapter 5—"How does the Boyfriend Within relate to a Boyfriend Without?"—considers some of the repercussions when dealing with others. Whether single, married, or dating, we all bring a host of expectations to the table. Consciously learning to locate our center of gravity within creates a personal revolution. We no longer require of our mates all sorts of inappropriate behavior for which they're not suited, or on which they haven't even been briefed. And we no longer look at being single as necessarily a lack, or failure. We learn to deal alertly with the world as it is, not as we think it should be. Formulaic scripts are tossed.

Chapter 6—"What's love got to do with it?"—presents one of the core concepts which can grow out of a deeper experience of the Boyfriend Within. We're used to thinking of love in romantic terms. Love is usually experienced as a sweet burning in the heart, accompanied by a great sense of well-being and self-satisfaction. Love makes us feel good about ourselves. But one of the mysteries of life is the way in which doing work (or "selfless service") for people we care about, or causes we care about, can also make our hearts burn within us. We can literally create the afterglow of love in ourselves by going on dates of personally meaningful volunteerism with the Boyfriend Within.

A great boon of the love and intimacy experienced in a good relationship, or in a functional family, is a *release* from some of the pain, stress, and alienation of our lives. To "come home" is to let down your guard a little, take off your tie, kick off your shoes, and let slip the mask, or masks, of persona applied during the day. But of course home is wherever you choose. You can turn your office into a temporary home by shutting the door and watching the sunset. Or your car, when you're driving along listening to a favorite book on tape.

Similarly you can create love and intimacy wherever you want. You can do so by learning to access your relationship to the Boyfriend Within. As the saying goes, home is where you hang your hat. Love and happiness can be found whenever, wherever, and however you allow yourself release from bad feelings, impermanent constraints, or contrived behavior. Some sessions will take more time and more unwinding; others, less.

A few weeks ago I visited a younger friend in the East Village. During a lull while he was changing a Metallica tape on his malfunctioning boom box, I eavesdropped on a couple of his twenty-something roommates discussing girl troubles in the next room. One of them said, "Well, my number one rule in dealing with women is just be yourself. I mean you can be a little bit more polite or more thoughtful than usual. But basically be yourself." His cliché rang through to me as so innocent . . . but also so inspiring, so true. He was the mouthpiece at that moment for a wise truth about dealing with the Boyfriend (or in his case, Girlfriend) Without.

I rediscovered the application of this truth for the Boyfriend Within for the dozenth time a few nights later. I'd had one of those days. It was late. I knew that to get my seven hours I needed to get to bed soon. But I was still churning, still having an imaginary conversation with an annoying magazine editor, and I was vexed about a trip that wasn't gelling. Luckily I decided to take some time for the Inner B: I put on

Chant; relaxed under a blanket on the couch, in a room lit by only a single candle. Within a half hour I was a happy camper. My worries were thankfully reduced to an appropriate scale of silly insignificance. I'd even figured out a structure for my next book, which had been eluding me for months. That is: I released *myself.* And I had done so by giving myself time and permission to just be myself, with myself. I'd adapted the twenty-something's advice for my own purposes.

I'm not saying that by bringing the Boyfriend Within into the conscious center of our lives we'll be *entirely* content. I have no idea where rich and successful fit into the picture, though I hope they're part of it. But I do believe that when we learn to find our Boyfriends Within, our hearts will become less restless. We'll tend to be happier.

In the words of Rumi: "Lovers don't finally meet somewhere / They're in each other all along."